D0426655

"This is the first genuine military biography of M. Kemal Ataturk ever written by anybody anywhere, including Turkey. As such, it fills a long neglected void, and it is an important work of original scholarship. Colonel Austin Bay lays a solid foundation for helping us understand the military career of this great commander. Well-researched and very readable—it is an essential read for those interested in this era or in the art of command."

—Edward J. Erickson, associate professor, Command and Staff College, Marine Corps University

"Kemal Ataturk is one of the great figures of the twentieth century. Austin Bay's delightfully written history reminds us why that is and why we will soon keenly miss Ataturk's influence."

—Glenn Reynolds, Beauchamp Brogan Distinguished Professor of Law, University of Tennessee, and author of the blog InstaPundit

"Bay's well-written book weaves the military, political, and personal strands of Ataturk's actions into an important story that has much to tell us about leadership. One of the compelling aspects of Bay's approach is that we see the world from Ataturk's point of view so that even a familiar event, like Gallipoli, appears in a new and fascinating way."

—Betty Sue Flowers, editor of *The Power of Myth*

The World Generals Series

"Palgrave's World Generals Series features great leaders whose reputations have transcended their own nations, whose bold characters led to new forms of combat, whose determination and courage gave shape to new dynasties and civilizations—men whose creativity and courage inspired multitudes. Beginning with illustrious World War II German Field Marshal Irwin Rommel, known as the Desert Fox, the series sheds new light on famous warrior-leaders such as Napoleon, Giap, Alexander, Julius Caesar, and Lafayette, drawing out the many important leadership lessons that are still relevant to our lives today."

—*General Wesley K. Clark (Ret.)*

This distinguished new series features the lives of eminent military leaders from around the world who changed history. Top military historians are writing concise but comprehensive biographies including the personal lives, battles, strategies, and legacies of these great generals, with the aim to provide background and insight into contemporary armies and wars, as well as to draw lessons for the leaders of today.

Rommel by Charles Messenger

Alexander the Great by Bill Yenne

Montgomery by Trevor Royle

Lafayette by Marc Leepson

Ataturk by Austin Bay

De Gaulle by Michael Haskew

Julius Caesar by Bill Yenne

Giap by James Warren

Ataturk

Lessons in Leadership from the Greatest General of the Ottoman Empire

Austin Bay

palgrave
macmillan

ATATURK

Copyright © Austin Bay, 2011.

First published in 2011 by
PALGRAVE MACMILLAN®
in the US—a division of St. Martin's Press LLC,
175 Fifth Avenue, New York, NY 10010.

Where this book is distributed in the UK, Europe and the rest of the world,
this is by Palgrave Macmillan, a division of Macmillan Publishers Limited,
registered in England, company number 785998, of Houndmills,
Basingstoke, Hampshire RG21 6XS.

Palgrave Macmillan is the global academic imprint of the above companies
and has companies and representatives throughout the world.

Palgrave® and Macmillan® are registered trademarks in the United States,
the United Kingdom, Europe and other countries.

ISBN: 978–0–230–10711–3

Library of Congress Cataloging-in-Publication Data

Bay, Austin.
    Ataturk : lessons in leadership from the greatest general of the Ottoman
Empire / Austin Bay; foreword by Wesley K. Clark.
        p. cm.
    Summary: "From a historian and former colonel in the U.S. Army
reserve, comes the remarkable biography of one of the founders of modern
Turkey"—Provided by publisher.
        ISBN 978–0–230–10711–3 (hardback)
        1. Ataturk, Kemal, 1881–1938. 2. Presidents—Turkey—Biography.
3. Kemalism. 4. Leadership. I. Title.

DR592.K4B27 2011
956.1′024092—dc22   2011002895
[B]

A catalogue record of the book is available from the British Library.

Design by Newgen Imaging Systems (P) Ltd., Chennai, India.

First edition: August 2011

10 9 8 7 6 5 4 3 2 1

Printed in the United States of America.

Contents

*Eight pages of black-and-white photos
appear between pages 94 and 95.*

Balkans and Eastern
Mediterranean, 1914

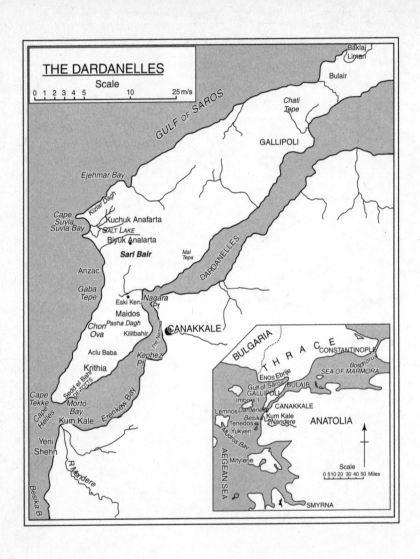

THE DARDANELLES

Scale

0 1 2 3 4 5   10   25 m/s

GULF OF SAROS

Báklaj Liman

Bulair

Chati Tepe

GALLIPOLI

Ejehmar Bay

Kizlar Dagh

Cape Suvla
Suvla Bay

Kuchuk Anafarta

SALT LAKE

Biyuk Analarta

Sari Bair

DARDANELLES

Mal Tepa

Anzac

Gaba Tepe

Eski Keru

Nagara Pt

Maidos

Pasha Dagh

Chon Ova

Kilitbahir

The Narrows

CANAKKALE

Aclu Baba

Kephez Pt

Krithia

Sedd el Bahr
DE-TOTTS

Erenkew Bay

Cape Tekke

Morto Bay

Cape Helles

Kum Kale

Yeni Shehn

R. Nendere

Besika B

Inset map

BULGARIA

T H R A C E

CONSTANTINOPLE

Bosphorus

SEA OF MARMORA

Enos Ebrile

Gulf of Saros

GALLIPOLI

BULAIR

Imbros I

Dardenelle

CANAKKALE

Lemnos

Besika

Tenedos

Kum Kale
Nandere

ANATOLIA

Yukyeri

Mitylene

Mudros Bay

AEGEAN SEA

Scale

0 5 10 20 30 40 50 Miles

SMYRNA

Acknowledgments

I WISH TO THANK THE DOZENS OF PEOPLE WHO HELPED ME WITH THIS project, but especially Laura Blake Peterson of Curtis Brown Ltd.; Dr. Edward Erickson and Dr. Richard DiNardo of the Marine Corps Command and Staff College (Quantico, Virginia); Laura Lancaster and Colleen Lawrie at Palgrave Macmillan; Elif Sevili; LTC Mesut Uyar, PhD (Turkish Military Academy, Ankara); Dr. Yuruk Iyriboz; Dr. Susan Shwartz; LTC Bruce Johnson; Kirk Spencer; Richard Kooris of 501 Studios; Gerald Robbins of the Foreign Policy Research Institute; and the lightning-fast interlibrary loan librarians at the University of Texas (Austin). Dr. Albert A. Nofi and Jim Dunnigan at StrategyPage.com provided their usual expert research advice; Colonel Kevin Smith and Colonel Sam Palmer added thoughtful encouragement. The biggest thanks are due my wife, Kathleen, and our daughters, Annabelle and Christiana, for their love and support.

Foreword

PROBABLY NO OTHER TWENTIETH-CENTURY LEADER DID MORE FOR HIS country than Mustafa Kemal Ataturk. He brought Turkey independence, changed its alphabet and culture, and created a secular democracy. And probably no twentieth-century general had any better battlefield instincts, skill, or discipline, proving himself under fire at every level of command. And certainly none so adroitly mixed revolutionary politics with military vision. Yet now, almost a century after his great achievements, he is nearly forgotten in the West, and even in Turkey his legacy is in dispute and his achievements threatened.

Austin Bay's fast moving biography of Ataturk explains the General Mustafa Kemal—who he was and how he did it. For it is the study of his character and development as a military leader that makes his later achievements as head of state understandable. To some American readers this may seem to be just a story set in a mystical land with unknown geography and foreign names. For readers elsewhere, though, Bay's crisp writing provides an easy entry into the more familiar story of war, courage, revolutionary change, and limitless possibilities every bit as current today as they were when these events occurred a century or more ago.

Ataturk was born in 1881 in Salonika, then part of the Ottoman Empire's extensive European holdings (now Thessaloniki in modern-day Greece). His family was of modest means, his father died when he was a boy, and his mother struggled financially. His mother expected him to be educated in classical Islam with the Koran, but young Mustafa felt at an early age that he was destined to be a soldier and pursued a Western education.

He grew up in a difficult and potentially insecure environment under constant challenge and threat, in the cauldron of a "clash of civilizations." At the time Salonika was a cosmopolitan seaport under Ottoman rule but threatened by Greek revanchism, pan-Slav nationalism, guerrilla conflict, and great power competition between Russia, Austria-Hungary, Germany, and Britain. The Ottoman Empire, once a mighty threat to European civilization, was beset by enemies on all sides, internal as well as external. Young Mustafa would have felt the pull and tug of all these cultural and political forces in his daily life.

Mustafa made his way from a prep school—where he was nearly perfect in his studies—into officer school. The army at the time was the most Westernized of the Ottoman institutions, struggling to adapt to Western technology and organizations in an effort to combat the mortal threat to the empire. And in a manner similar to any ambitious youngster in the military, he worked his way up the ranks. He studied assiduously, impressed mentors, and schemed for the most enhancing assignments. He was one among many talented, ambitious young officers marked for some degree of success.

However Mustafa had qualities that most of his contemporaries lacked. First, he had a broader vision. While Western militaries teach the subordination of the soldier to the state, Mustafa and a few of his contemporaries saw beyond the military as a career and sought to use it as a vehicle to promote far wider modernization. Second, he was incredibly determined, to the point of arrogance, and almost without personal regard for his popularity, safety, or well-being in pursuit of larger aims. Third, he had superb judgment about people, publicity, and political forces. He was smart and wise, even from an early age. Altogether for the sultan he was a very dangerous young man, for the sultan was well aware of the incipient threat posed by a modernizing, Western-influenced military.

In a variety of assignments prior to World War I, he met and attempted to work with the slightly older Young Turks already scheming to overthrow the Porte. He experienced the clash of arms, saw irregular conflict at close range, and noticed the pervasive corruption and slack in Ottoman forces, thieving over the very people they were supposed to protect. He was forceful, outspoken, and effective— and not surprisingly he made enemies even among his fellow reform-minded coconspirators. He had a brush with the secret police; he was given unpromising assignments, sent far from the seats of influence and points of conflict. Yet he came through each challenge with enhanced personal reputation as well as new skills and capabilities. He could lead, plan, negotiate, compromise. He could brief privately and speak publicly. And he advanced in rank and responsibility.

As World War I engulfed Europe, the Ottoman Empire was dragged into the war and became a target of Allied forces. Stalemated in Western Europe trench-style warfare, the Brits saw the Dardanelles and passage into the Black Sea as their most promising opportunity to split the Central Powers—Germany and Austria-Hungary—from their new Ottoman ally and link forces through southeast Europe with the czar's forces. It was a young Winston Churchill, then first lord of the admiralty, who pushed the Brits into seeking an amphibious invasion of the Gallipoli Peninsula to overrun the critical Dardanelles–Bosporus and open up the sea route to Russia.

Mustafa Kemal, thirty-four years old, was on the other side commanding a division of Turkish soldiers, facing the greatest forces in the world. He moved to the scene, personally intervened to stop a Turkish retreat, and ordered his battalions into a desperate defensive action to hold the decisive high ground overlooking the enemy beachhead. A solitary figure on a hilltop looking out with binoculars, directing a battle of one brigade, then two brigades, then four brigades—over the next days and weeks Ataturk was given command of increasingly larger, more capable formations, and for critical months he blunted, held off, and ultimately defeated the invasion.

Western commentaries of Gallipoli often fault their own commanders for delay and hesitancy on the beachhead. And there was some of that. But war is a head-to-head struggle. And the Ottoman forces, personally led and inspired in this critical battle, were tougher, more resilient, and capable at the decisive point. Mustafa Kemal Ataturk had won one of the greatest battles of World War I.

Ataturk's later military exploits are faithfully recounted as he moved upward in rank and responsibility, holding eastern Anatolia in a little-reported campaign against significant Russian forces and later fighting against Allenby in Syria. And then he parlayed his battlefield skills and energy into positions of ever-higher leadership—even as he was forced out of uniform by a devastated sultanate suffering under the British occupation.

By now he had earned the leadership and respect of all within the Ottoman military. He led forces against the British supported Greeks and cleared the boundaries of present-day Turkey.

In other armies today, across the remains of the Ottoman Empire, young officers are wrestling with the competing demands of politics and the military. They seek to use their military background and connections to bring about political change and reform. Austin Bay's account of Ataturk provides perhaps the best lens through wish to view the struggles ahead, as many others seek to attempt to do or to reverse what Mustafa Kemal Ataturk did.

—General Wesley K. Clark (Ret.)

Winning Time

His presence changed everything.

"*Ingiliz, Ingiliz!*" The fleeing men of the Ottoman Ninth Division yelled as Lieutenant Colonel Mustafa Kemal appeared on the rough mountain peak with the dominating view of Gallipoli's European battleground and the Dardanelles's Asian shore.[1] Kemal, with the lead regiment of his own Nineteenth Division still a desperate ten minutes behind him, paused as the panicked Ninth Division soldiers clambered about him. With a snapped order he immediately halted their retreat, and they steadied. When he asked the soldiers why they fled, they pointed back at their pursuers, the darting-here-and-there files of British Commonwealth infantry wearing brown Australian slouch hats and bearing Enfield .303 rifles. With quick steps the young commander crossed the rock outcrop and then stood perfectly erect. It was a calculated act of exposure—as the leader, he had the responsibility to see and assess, and then decide the next course of action. He peered down the rough slope. On this clear, bright April morning in 1915, the Australians pressed forward, climbing upward and eastward from the marl beach where they had made their dawn landing. Ascending the dry, knife-edge ridges and threading the steep yellow gullies that rose from the Aegean Sea to the Gallipoli peninsula's central Sari Bair massif, they fought the rugged mountain now as well as erratic fire from scattered Turkish riflemen.

From that rock precipice, near a solitary tree, the thirty-three-year-old Kemal, with a taciturn face, pale complexion, and ice-blue eyes, saw the immediate dilemma and linked it to potential outcomes.[2] The Aussie infantry's hard slog up the *nullahs,* the ravines running from the Ariburnu cove on the Aegean coast to the peak of Chunuk Bair, foreshadowed a manifold horror that Kemal intended to stop. The minutes that unfolded, here and now, on this mountain, would shape subsequent decades. The tactical battles for the ridge system, the bitter, close-quarter rifle and bayonet fights between tired Australians and frightened Turks, were of immense strategic consequence—immediately for Turkey and eventually for the entire world.

✠

A few weeks earlier, Allied warships had tried to smash their way through the Dardanelles Strait. They shelled the fort of Kumkale in Asia Minor, near the site of ancient Troy, and the forts on Cape Helles, at the peninsula's southern tip. Then the battleships dared to enter the crossfire of the Narrows, where carefully sown and protected Ottoman naval mines ripped their hulls. Several sank with catastrophic loss of life. To breach the Dardanelles, the French and British fleets needed soldiers to destroy the coastal guns so that their slow and vulnerable minesweepers could clear the mines and lead the warships through the channel.[3]

After the fleet retreated, Ottoman and German spies observed Allied troop ships loading in eastern Mediterranean ports. The Ottoman Fifth Army defending the peninsula and its German commander, General Otto Liman von Sanders, expected a British and French amphibious assault. Where and when the Allied force would land on the peninsula sparked heated debate among Ottoman and German officers.

April 25 provided the answers, as battleships and cruisers bombarded Turkish positions up and down the peninsula. The Allies were back, this time with infantry divisions determined to crack the Dardanelles. Allied commanders knew their Gallipoli assault was a strategic gamble, but a gamble with war-winning potential. On the Western front, the mobile war of August 1914 had come to a deadly, indecisive halt as the stymied Allied and German armies both constructed a flankless trench and fortification system running from the Swiss border through France to the English Channel. Courageous and increasingly desperate frontal attacks failed to break this reinforced defensive line. Massed infantry assaults against dug-in machine guns and relentless artillery slugfests produced horrifying casualties but no territorial gain. As the death toll climbed and one terrible day of fruitless attrition warfare followed another, political and military leaders sought alternatives. Could mobility and maneuverability be restored, possibly in another geographic theater of war? The Allies with their sea-dominating navies considered the great straits on continental Europe's southeastern flank. The Gallipoli Peninsula, a rocky thread of Europe, extends southwest from eastern Thrace and separates the upper Aegean Sea from the Dardanelles. Senior strategists argued that storming the Dardanelles, taking the Ottoman capital of Constantinople on the Sea of Marmara, and then advancing through the Bosporus (the strait leading from the Sea of Marmara to the Black Sea) would restore strategic mobility as well as secure a maritime supply route to their eastern ally, Russia. This strategic coup might break the trench-war deadlock in France. Seizing the entire straits zone (from the Aegean Sea to the Black Sea) would effectively knock the Ottoman Empire out of the war, further isolating the German and Austro-Hungarian empires.

The naval gunfire hammering the coastline and hills signaled a renewed assault on the Dardanelles and alerted Kemal and his Nineteenth Division. Ninth Ottoman Division units not already committed to coastal defense also began to respond. The first wave of the Australian and New Zealand Army Corps (ANZAC) had hit the Ariburnu beach at 4:30 A.M. and engaged the Ninth Division's forward-deployed riflemen. Excited reports from Cape Helles confirmed other Anglo-French landings. Luck and the new division commander's rigorous training regimen had the Nineteenth Division's Fifty-seventh Regiment awake, armed, and standing in formation near the village of Bigali, just north of the Dardanelles port of Maidos. Kemal had a ready strike force, and for two frustrating hours he sought guidance from his corps command. Finally, he acted on his own authority: he ordered the Fifty-seventh Regiment to follow him to the mountain peaks.[4]

Chunuk Bair, the peak where Kemal met the Ninth Division's fleeing troops, Battleship Hill below it, and Hill 971 above it split the Gallipoli Peninsula. From Chunuk Bair, a man using military binoculars can see in detail the historic strait separating Thrace from Anatolia. Combat forces holding the Hill 971–Chunuk Bair–Battleship Hill escarpment would dominate the central Gallipoli Peninsula, making it the key position between the fortress town of Boyalir (Bulair) at the peninsula's northern end and Cape Helles. Kemal knew that an army that possessed the peninsula would control the Dardanelles. With the strait's defenses breached, British and French battleships could thread the slender throat of the Narrows, cross the Sea of Marmara, and bombard Constantinople. The Australian soldiers attacking uphill were the human spearhead of this multifaceted Allied military and political operation. The great fleets and armies following the advancing line of Aussie riflemen posed a fatal threat to the entire Ottoman Empire. Halting them here and now would buy time to gather reinforcements, to counterattack, and to defeat the Allies' bold scheme.

Kemal and his soldiers had arrived on the dominating heights. Now, in a span of precious seconds, they directly confronted the Allies' calculated bid to crack the peninsula's defensive spine. Rifle against rifle, bayonet to bayonet, fought on naked rock and in narrow gullies—a fierce, close battle was imminent and its outcome of decisive import.

Kemal later insisted that the ridges' critical location and his analysis of Ottoman defensive preparations during the First Balkan War informed what he regarded as an obvious decision. Kemal believed that any professionally prepared and responsible officer would promptly grasp the Sari Bair massif's military significance. Upon receiving intelligence that enemy forces had landed below the hills, the responsible officer should act, not wait for orders. He should immediately go to the critical sector or position, swiftly assess the situation, and then direct operations to defeat the enemy. To borrow Kemal's own trenchant metaphor for military insight and foresight, he fought Gallipoli's first hours with binoculars, not a sword.[5] A pair of binoculars serves as an apt military metaphor for strategic insight and foresight. The commander possessing these gifts of visualization comprehensively assesses the current situation then postulates and analyzes (often with astonishing mental speed) potential actions and reactions through time. His goal is obtaining advantage over the enemy in order to achieve favorable ends. His insight pierces the immediate present's chaos and confusion and identifies military, political, social, and even psychological opportunities others cannot see; his foresight anticipates future circumstances, which he will shape and create by actions (operations, in military jargon). The truly gifted strategic leader—the genius—fosters conditions for successful future operations directed by other leaders over an extended period of time. The genius influences and shapes events for decades and perhaps centuries.

Ataturk was this kind of leader. His extraordinary career as a soldier-statesman provides numerous lessons in foresight, multifaceted visualization, complex analysis, and unified action—all of it backed by determined physical and moral courage.

The immediate crisis on Chunuk Bair required raw courage.

"Why are you running away?" Kemal asked.

"The enemy, sir..." the retreating Ninth Division soldiers said.

"Where?"

"Over there," they replied, pointing toward Battleship Hill.

Sure enough, an enemy line was advancing. The enemy troops were already closer to Kemal than the forward element of his own Fifty-seventh Regiment approaching from the eastern slope. He did not know whether reason or intuition compelled him. He turned to the retreating soldiers and said, "You mustn't run away from the enemy."

"We've no more ammunition left," they replied.

"If you've got no ammunition, you have your bayonets."

He ordered them to fix bayonets and lie flat on the ground. As he did, the enemy also lay down. The Ottomans had won time.[6]

Kemal's impromptu deception worked. The Aussies saw the Turks stop, turn, and hit the ground. To experienced infantrymen these acts in sequence signaled an ambush; fixing bayonets indicated offensive esprit, and that bold display sold the ruse. Within minutes the lead battalion of the Fifty-seventh Regiment arrived, and the Ottoman retreat was over. Turning toward his regiment, Kemal issued his most famous order:

"I do not expect you to attack, I order you to die! In the time which passes until we die, other troops and commanders can take our place!"[7]

The Turkish counterattack commenced at 10:24 A.M. and with it began the history-making ascendance of Mustafa Kemal Ataturk.

❖

The ability to see how a minute may resonate through decades—and, despite grave danger, act with intent to achieve goals—is a sign of what Prussian general and strategic theorist Carl von Clausewitz called "military genius."

By genius Clausewitz meant "a very highly developed mental aptitude for a particular occupation." Surveying "those gifts of mind and temperament that in combination bear on military activity,"[8] he emphasized that courage "in the face of personal danger, and courage to accept responsibility" are required. "The highest kind of courage is a compound" of "indifference to danger" and "positive motives as ambition, patriotism, and enthusiasm."[9]

Clausewitz believed that war requires intellect of a special type, for "during an operation decisions have usually to be made at once; there may be no time to review a situation or even to think it through." For the combat leader, "if the mind is to emerge unscathed from this relentless struggle with the unforeseen, two qualities are indispensable: first, an intellect, that even in the darkest hour, retains some glimmerings of the inner light which leads to truth; and second, the courage to follow this faint light wherever it may lead. The first of these qualities is described by the French term, *coup d'oeil;* the second is determination."[10]

Clausewitz's *coup d'oeil* referred to both the "physical" and "inward eye," but, "stripped of metaphor, . . . the concept merely refers to the quick recognition of a truth that the mind would ordinarily miss or would perceive only after long study and reflection."[11]

❖

Biographers and historians tend to focus on Ataturk's achievements as a statesman and fail to recognize his military achievements, particularly those in Turkey's War of Independence.[12]

Recent events in the eastern Mediterranean and Middle East, however, have sparked an Ataturk Renaissance. Ataturk has never disappeared as a subject of Turkish personal fascination and public political struggle. In 1997, *Time* magazine ran an Internet-based poll asking readers to name the person of the century; pro-Ataturk Turkish voters swamped the website.[13] On other occasions the popular Western press has recognized Ataturk's achievements. During his January 1, 2000, broadcast, *McLaughlin Group* host John McLaughlin declared that his award for "the Person of the Full Millennium goes to Mustafa Kemal Ataturk, a Muslim visionary who, in 1922, abolished the Ottoman sultanate, a feudal monarchy; emancipated women; adopted Western dress; converted the Arabic alphabet to Latin—the only leader in history to successfully turn a Muslim nation into a Western parliamentary democracy and secular state."[14]

Of course, such an accolade is outrageous: The second millennium AD had thousands of people whose global legacies influenced centuries of history—take as two very different examples Genghis Khan and Shakespeare. But—granting the commentator's intentional extravagance—McLaughlin gives an answer backed by evidence and twelve hundred years of conflict. Ataturk's revolution bridged Islam and Christendom, Europe and Asia, and continues to affect the developing world, including South Asia, Africa, and South America. His revolution fostered conditions that began to resolve Eurasian conflicts rooted in the fifteenth century, when the Ottomans finally destroyed the Byzantine Empire. The fifteenth century may understate the case. Asian and Arabian invaders had vexed the Byzantine Empire (which was once the eastern half of the Roman Empire) since the middle of the first millennium.

Twenty-first-century wars also directly involve Ataturk and his legacy. Polemics that Osama bin Laden delivered before and after the 9/11 terror attacks mention "eighty years" of Muslim indignation. Bin Laden's eighty years refer to Ataturk's social, economic, and political modernization programs that replaced sclerotic Ottoman institutions, in particular the Islamic caliphate. In republican Turkey, a state with an overwhelmingly Muslim population, Ataturk systematically detached the government from the Muslim clergy; an elected parliament's legislated law ruled the nation, not Islamic sharia. For this al-Qaeda despises Ataturk.

Although this book focuses on Kemal Ataturk's military career, he also understood and mastered the interconnectedness of politics. Ataturk practiced Clausewitz's observation that "war is not merely an act of policy, but a true political instrument, a continuation of political intercourse, carried on with other means."[15] Practicing interconnected politics requires integrating the military, diplomatic, economic, and informational elements of power. This makes cleanly dividing Ataturk's military exploits and political endeavors all but impossible, and even if one could, it would be a mistake. His talents encompassed all levels of conflict, from the tactical through the operational to the strategic, and even into the rarified realm of grand strategy. His tactical experience included conventional battle and guerrilla warfare. He was a successful operational-level commander on Gallipoli's Anafartalar front and with the Sixteenth Corps in 1916. His strategic-level military and political leadership during the Turkish War of Independence, waged while simultaneously engaging Europe's great powers in a diplomatic struggle over the Treaty of Sèvres, was brilliant.

And his enemies knew it. Ataturk won over his Greek antagonist (and the political author of Greece's disastrous Ionian venture), the prime minister of Greece during World War I, Eleftherios Venizelos. It was Venizelos who in 1934 nominated Ataturk for the Nobel Peace Prize.[16] Ataturk understood that the transition from war-fighting to peacemaking and subsequently the maintenance of peace were integral to achieving his grand strategic aims in the complex global system. In 1923, following the War of Independence, Ataturk and Venizelos negotiated an exchange of populations between "lost territories," which stabilized Thrace and the Aegean coast. Though the exchange still embitters extremists in both nations, it prevented incessant guerrilla activity and community slaughter, ultimately saving tens of thousands of lives. Ataturk, the war-winning president, renounced any desire to recover his own hometown, Salonika (Greek Thessaloniki). This added immense, personal moral power to the exchange agreement. The victor sacrificed for peace—the act of a statesman, not a conqueror.

Ataturk integrated combat operations with other political action while accounting for social and cultural forces. Today the US Joint Chiefs of Staff uses the term "unified action" to describe this synergism of diplomacy, economics, military power, and information power.[17] The term is dry and bureaucratic, but the fusion of thought, power, and action that it describes requires a combination of skill, intellectual expertise, psychological and diplomatic deftness, and personal confidence in command that few statesmen have ever possessed.

Ataturk had that combination, and he used it repeatedly. In an article published in 1960 titled "Swords and Plowshares: The Turkish Army as a Modernizing Force," Daniel Lerner and Richard Robinson argue that after the War of Independence, Kemal saw "the military victory he had won was only a temporary reprieve." To secure Turkey, they wrote,

> would require a total revolution in a relatively short period of time. A modern military establishment was clearly impossible without modern science and industry. These...were clearly impossible without a transformed political and social system which would permit the people of Turkey to realize more fully their human potential. Illiteracy, debilitating disease, religious dogma and fatalism, subordination of women—all of these had

to go.... The process of dramatic reform... was set in motion, each individual move being carefully timed and designed to take full advantage of favorable turns of events. Insight, inscrutability, and a sense of timing were among Ataturk's great assets as a radical planner.[18]

Military campaign studies of this great general should consider these dimensions and their dynamic implications, for Ataturk considered them as he planned the campaigns, fought the battles, and prepared for future action.

CHAPTER 1

Rumelia

AN ASTUTE YOUNG MAN WITH MILITARY APTITUDE LIVING IN LATE nineteenth-century Macedonia could hear the violent rumors in Salonika's streets, examine a map of the seaport's Balkan backcountry, and swiftly conclude that with every passing day this crumbling European edge of the Ottoman Empire presented leaders with difficult decisions, each one charged with strategic consequence.

Mustafa was born in 1881 in Salonika, then, as now, the northern Aegean's principal seaport and commercial center. At times in the late nineteenth century Salonika's thriving business district, enchanting neighborhoods and polyglot sophistication might beguilingly mask the nationalist rivalries and fierce ethnic resentments dividing Balkan Greeks, Bulgarians, Albanians, and Turks. However, the imposing men in impressive uniforms trudging through the city's streets—soldiers assigned to the Ottoman army's substantial garrison—were sent there for a reason.

Since the end of the seventeenth century—with the Ottoman defeat at Vienna in 1683 an indelible mark—military failure, political sclerosis, and cultural decay had sapped the empire. Ambassadors and editorialists employed a biting quip to describe Turkey's slow decline, calling it "the sick man of Europe."[1] Muslims, regarding Islam as God's final revelation, wondered "what went wrong?" with history.[2] They looked to the Ottoman state, as defender of the caliphate in Constantinople, to reassert Islam's spiritual and political superiority. Observing the technological creativity of Europe and the global reach of "Western powers," Ottoman sultans and their Sublime Porte ministers pondered the decline.[3]

A few innovators sought answers beyond calls to revive the Ottoman martial spirit and recover the Islamic virtues that had empowered the Prophet.[4] Eighteenth-century viziers hired Western military advisers and bought Western arms; the empire came to depend on imported experts and technology. Nineteenth-century Ottoman reformers, recognizing the ascendancy of European educational paradigms, established a two-track and centralized state school system, with military academies (*askeri*) to train officers and civil service schools (*mulki*) to educate civilian administrators. Thus, Turkish military schools offered young men with talent a fine education and a route to a prestigious career. The military took students from preparatory schools to military high schools (usually co-located with major military headquarters), and then to the premier institution, Istanbul's Harbiye, the war college.[5] Officers produced by this system became the empire's schooled elite, militarily proficient and technologically savvy soldiers also prepared for an array of diplomatic assignments and advisory posts. The sultan and his viziers expected these "new men" would halt their empire's decay and fossilization.

Military life and its challenges attracted young Mustafa, as did the Ottoman army's educational and social opportunities. Fastidious with his grooming, deliberate with his personal appearance, the blond, fair-complected boy with blue eyes admired the dash of army uniforms. "I was born a soldier," Ataturk later claimed he told his mother, Zubeyde, after an argument. "I shall die a soldier."[6]

Mustafa's father, Ali Riza, a civil servant who dabbled in Macedonia's lumber trade, died in 1888 when Mustafa was seven, leaving Zubeyde a twenty-seven-year-old widow.[7] For several years he had suffered from a series of illnesses, including tuberculosis exacerbated by depression and alcoholism. Three of Zubeyde's five children had already died in childhood. Mustafa and his sister, Makbule, were her cherished survivors.[8]

Despite Mustafa's keen interest in military service, his mother required convincing. Zubeyde opposed her son's ambition. She feared for his life, and also respected traditional Muslim schooling. But Ali had strongly favored a broad education for his son. The education question that divided their home reflected a debate playing out on a larger scale between European liberal concepts and conventional Muslim values. Early on Ali and Zubeyde had argued over Mustafa's studies. "My first memory of my childhood concerns the problem of my schooling," Ataturk said in 1922. "There was a deep struggle between my mother and father concerning this."[9] As a civil servant, Ali saw the value of "the new manner" of liberal and technologically informed European education that Ottoman civil service and military schools emphasized. The formidable Zubeyde preferred Mustafa attend a more traditional Koranic school that emphasized religious education. In her opinion, piety as well as neighborhood prestige required it.

The violence in the hills outside her home city of Salonika sharpened Zubeyde's maternal objections. A cosmopolitan veneer of peace, with its busy wharves and glossy lamplit cafes, blessed the seaport. In bars like the Olympos, Yonyo, and Kristal (favorites of Turkish officers and cadets), Greeks and Bulgars mixed with Italian sailors, Levantine merchants, Sephardic Jews, and other local Macedonians, sharing cigarettes, nibbling mezes, drinking coffee, beer, and harsh, high-octane *raki* served by Christian girls or waiters from the Greek quarter near the piers. Physically and culturally, late nineteenth-century Salonika combined Ottoman polyglot exoticism and European commercial activism. The Ottoman capital, Constantinople, bridged Asia and Europe. Though Turkish, Salonika was Europe, a backwater town compared to Berlin and Paris, but an intellectual center for Turkish modernizers. In 1889, new train tracks connected Salonika to the European rail system.[10] Trade goods moved more efficiently than ever; people moved more easily; the speed of information transmission and evaluation, particularly financial and political, increased.

Salonika's backcountry, however, was Europe's most troubled corner: the Balkans. In the 1890s, as young Mustafa argued with his mother, nationalist aspirations, ethnic grudges, and historical grievances had once again primed the Balkan powder keg. Groups of resentful Macedonian Greeks and Slavs—one moment smugglers, the next guerrillas, by morning mere peasants and laborers—roamed the hinterland, their clandestine activities vexing Ottoman police.[11] Intelligence officers knew that violence in the hills by *comitadjis* (partisan bands) foreshadowed agitation in the cities; if unchecked by force, guerrilla bands became revolutionary armies. Serbia had slipped the "Ottoman yoke" following this script, as had Greece.[12] Throughout the Ottoman Empire, but especially in Rumelia, the region encompassing Thrace and Ottoman southeastern Europe,[13] guerrillas, religious friction, ethnic clashes, land claims, and nationalist schemes eventually led to war, and in war soldiers died. Economic change stoking historical animosities and technological change challenging cultural traditions produced enormous political stress. The sultan's ministers saw the trends, and they worried; Zubeyde, a widow with a sole surviving son, did as well.

Historic grievance and ethnic animus intertwined with geopolitical interests. Greek leaders eyed Salonika and the whole of Macedonia. So did Bulgaria. Greek nationalists argued that reclaiming Macedonia furthered the cause of Greek liberation from Turkish domination. Thessalonica (named for Alexander the Great's half-sister), had served as Greek Macedonia's chief port; Byzantine Greek Thessalonica was a major trading and cultural center. The Bulgarians believed that acquiring Salonika provided them with a prized strategic asset: a Mediterranean port. If Salonika belonged to Bulgaria, Bulgarian global shipping could avoid the Ottoman-controlled Bosporus and Dardanelles.

✦

Zubeyde and Ali eventually agreed to a ceremonial arrangement—literally—with regard to Mustafa's education. In 1888, before his father's death, Mustafa attended a neighborhood Muslim school long enough to learn a few Koranic verses and parade through the neighborhood with his Koranic teacher. His wife's traditionalism appeased, Ali transferred his seven-year-old son to a primary school that focused on basic education.[14] The clothes-conscious Mustafa, however, recalled he still had to wear "baggy oriental trousers, tied with a sash."[15] Then Ali died. Widowed in a patriarchal society, Zubeyde moved her family to a farm owned by a relative. After haphazardly enrolling her son in rural schools, Zubeyde sent Mustafa back to Salonika, where he first attended a *mulki*.

Mustafa's experience ended awkwardly. Following a vigorous disagreement with a teacher, which led to a beating, and with the help of a Major Kadri, an army officer living in Salonika,[16] the resolute twelve-year-old conspired to take the entrance exam to Salonika's military middle school (the Selanik Askeri Rustiyesi). He passed it and enrolled.

A dream ended the educational dispute with his mother and confirmed his choice of a military career. Zubeyde claimed that in a dream she "saw her son sitting on a golden tray on the top of a minaret. Running to the foot of the minaret, she heard a voice intoning, "If you allow your son to go to military school, he shall remain high up here. If you do not he shall be thrown down."[17] Zubeyde's dream may have been apocryphal, an after-the-fact folktale adding stardust and magic to the hero's legacy, though she insisted the dream occurred. Whatever the source of her dream, divine inspiration or retrospective projection, her son did indeed reach the pinnacle of his profession.

Mustafa loved the military school's books and martial atmosphere, especially the distinction of a soldier's uniform. For him, the uniform conveyed more than rising public status and individual stature. Freed from sash and pantaloons, the immaculately groomed young man took pride in his new appearance. Family acquaintances recalled Mustafa presented a striking figure, a precocious youth comfortable when engaging neighborhood adults in discussions, his chin raised, his fair hair combed, his hands in his uniform's European-cut pants pockets.

No doubt Ataturk's adult successes added shine and color to this and similar memories of his childhood. However, throughout her life, Makbule recounted (to her own amusement) stories of her brother's demanding concern for his personal presentation as well as his teenage flirtations. Clothes do not make the man, but they certainly enhance the impression. Vain, young Mustafa's subsequent career demonstrates that he understood the political effects of an authoritative, elegant, and dominating personal impression.[18]

※

Kemal means "perfect" in Turkish.[19] How Mustafa got his famous nickname, "Mustafa the Perfect," remains a matter of speculation and debate. In Turkish tradition, an elder may give a young person a nickname to serve as a permanent second name.[20] One story says Ataturk's mathematical brilliance so impressed a preparatory school instructor that the teacher dubbed him Kemal. Many commentators question this tale's particulars and they suggest the teacher bestowed the second name merely to distinguish Mustafa from a classmate with the same name.[21] Quite possibly young Mustafa selected the name himself, "as a tribute to the patriotic poet Namik Kemal," whose poetry and plays influenced him intellectually and politically.[22]

Kemal did well at the military preparatory school. Before he graduated, however, however, his mother remarried. He appreciated his mother's social and economic situation. A widow's life was difficult, and her new husband, Ragip, proved to be a kind and generous man. However, a new man heading up the household tested Kemal's pride; the only son decided to move in with a relative. In 1895 he graduated fourth in his class. Salonika's military high school was the logical next step, but at the recommendation of several teachers, Mustafa chose to attend the school in Monastir, Macedonia,[23] as a boarding student. Monastir put distance between him and his step-father. Still, via the railroad, Kemal could quickly return to Salonika to see friends, family, and, according to Makbule, infatuated girlfriends.

Monastir was a polyglot provincial town of 37,000, with Greek, Slav, and Albanian communities. Location and demographics placed it in a cauldron. With Serbia and Bulgaria close by and the Greek frontier to the south, Monastir's military headquarters played a central role in Ottoman security plans for western Macedonia. Monastir's Ottoman pashas (generals) knew their neighbors regarded the town as disputed territory. Bulgaria had taken it from the Byzantine Greeks and controlled it from the eighth to eleventh centuries, when the Byzantines reconquered the town. It exchanged hands repeatedly until the Ottomans took control in 1382.

In 1895, despite new military preparations, Ottoman control of western Macedonia was insistently challenged. Cadets attending the military high school saw the situation and the stakes. A dirty war simmered in nearby mountains and valleys. Greek and Slav guerrilla raids increased; Turkish partisans formed guerrilla bands, some cast as local militia auxiliaries. In the Aegean Sea, a larger, more dangerous war between old antagonists attracted international attention, particularly in Great Britain and France. In 1897 Greek inhabitants of Crete, with the aid of mainland Greek nationalists, began a "war of liberation" for their island.[24] Greece and the Ottoman Empire's forces clashed in Macedonia, as Greek partisan fighters crossed the frontier. The Ottoman government responded by strengthening its forces throughout Rumelia.

Macedonia, the Balkan front line, attracted army volunteers from every corner of the empire. Their patriotic marches and demonstrations in Monastir deeply affected the academy students. Mustafa and another cadet tried to enlist in the army to fight and went so far as to attempt to leave the school. That fling failed when an official recognized the cadets and sent them back.[25] Ottoman forces in Macedonia defeated the Greek attacks, but Crete was another matter. Though ostensibly remaining under Ottoman control, Crete acquired local autonomy. Many Cretan Muslims fled the island, some relocating to the Ottoman North African province of Tripolitania (Libya).

In the best schools the best students learn from one another. Ataturk credited several cadets at Monastir with opening intellectual and political vistas for him. Omer Naci, a poet, recommended books, which Ataturk said introduced him to literature. Fellow Macedonian (and lifelong professional and personal friend) Ali Fethi, spoke superb French, and Mustafa admired his worldliness. Ali possessed a political mind, one looking west for philosophical models, with the French Enlightenment a particular interest. Ali encouraged Ataturk to read Comte, Montesquieu, Voltaire, and Rousseau.[26] These philosophers and the French Revolution informed both men's analysis of their troubled present. The Ottoman Empire of 1898, however, was not the France of 1792, though the French had confronted a decaying, absolute monarchy. The Reign of Terror and its guillotine shattered their revolution, and in the murderous vortex a military leader took control. Napoleon, ultimately shedding the guise of liberator, crowned himself emperor, then waged war from Egypt to Spain to Moscow, his warpath ending at Waterloo. Was there another, more just, more permanent, conceivably less destructive path to modernity for a Muslim empire who had no Voltaire? Could a constructive Napoleon exist?

CHAPTER 2

Young Turks

In November 1898, at the age of eighteen, Mustafa Kemal graduated from the Monastir academy. He ranked second in his class. His scholastic achievement and leadership ability assured him a place in Constantinople's War College, located in the Ottoman capital's most cosmopolitan quarter, Pera.[1] Built on the European residential borough's heights above the Bosporus, the War College abutted Pera's central Taksim Square and the imperial garrison's Stone Barracks. An imposing, yellow-brick, Turkish-Renaissance compound, the barracks housed imperial guard units charged with protecting the grandest palace, the Dolmabahce, and, to the north within quick marching distance via streets threading the ridges, the reigning Sultan Abdulhamid II's secluded Yildiz Palace.

In March 1899 Kemal entered the War College's infantry class. Like other cadets arriving from provincial academies, he immediately encountered Pera's steep streets, fashionable boulevards, and the seductive nightlife of notorious taverns and cabarets.

Pera, Greek for "beyond," began as a reference to the Thracian hills beyond the Golden Horn estuary north of Constantinople. For foreign sophisticates and urbane Ottomans, it was a delightful Eurasian spectacle of luxury apartments and fancy shops. It was Constantinople with a distinctive pulse, a thriving, indulgent Turkish world existing beyond the repressive doctrinal command of the caliphate. Fifteenth-century economics and demographics had fostered Pera's unique status. After Constantinople fell in 1453 to Mehmet the Conqueror, Pera became the more or less official residence of Greek, Venetian, and Genoan traders, as well as for an international cohort of talented foreigners with the business links and technological skills the expanding empire required.[2]

Abdulhamid II's late nineteenth-century empire, however, was shrinking. Officers and cadets educated in the military's European-influenced education system blamed his fossilized institutions and politics. To Ottoman modernizers, Pera's social and economic amalgam demonstrated the potential vitality of a liberalized Eurasian civilization.

Ottoman military elites, Turks schooled on Europe's technological, cultural, and educational advances, argued for systemic revitalization. In 1889, students at the Military Medical College (also located in Pera) decided the empire required revolutionary change. They formed a clandestine society, the Ottoman Union. Revolutionary political reform demanded secrecy; the sultan's police were on the lookout for dissent, particularly in the military. Kings and dictators are always wary of their security forces; autocrats rely on them for protection and enforcement, but a jealous general can launch a coup. The sultan's situation was ironic since the military and civil service were his approved agents of modernization. The sultan wanted a technologically modern force, but modernity requires more than gadgetry—ultimately people must learn to use the new technology.

The advent of new technology entails learning new information that in turn compels the social system to adapt, even if ever so subtly.[3] For centuries the empire had imported experts, but foreigners brought potentially compromising political entanglements and threatened cultural changes.

Creating and manning a technologically modern, self-reliant Ottoman army required improving and modernizing the education system. The military education system itself was an example of information modernization on an institutional scale. Informed officers were exposed to new social ideas, and this broader access to information suggested the need for liberalized political policies. A similar process had occurred in Western Europe. The advent of the printing press had magnified Martin Luther's challenge to the pope, and in later centuries scientists evaluating astronomical, geological, and zoological evidence disputed literal interpretations of the Christian and Hebrew Bibles. German philologists using linguistic and anthropological methods noted similarities between biblical stories and Sumerian myths. Might Allah's final revelation, the Koran, the foundation of the caliphate, face similar scrutiny? The sultan's spies had to watch closely and occasionally act to cull potential troublemakers, lest at some tipping point the human social adaptations that the new technology engendered were to produce revolutionary political change.

In 1895 the medical students' secret society was renamed the Committee for Union and Progress (CUP, İttihat ve Terakki Cemiyeti). Ottoman reformers joined and radical exile groups in Europe, particularly in Paris and Geneva, made common cause with the CUP. In 1896 the medical school dissidents attempted a coup. The police exposed it and the effort flopped; its leaders were arrested, convicted, and exiled.[4]

Reformist ideas, however, continued to motivate the cadets studying in early twentieth-century Pera. Kemal, honing his French, the "language of culture and progress," devoured French newspapers.[5]

Their articles, essays, and reviews reflected the broad cultural and intellectual parameters of European liberal constitutionalism.

Ataturk recalled in an interview, "During the years at the War College political ideas emerged. We were still unable to gain real insight into the situation. It was the period of Abdulhamid. We were reading the books of Namik Kemal. Surveillance was tight. Most of the time we found the chance to read only in the barracks after going to bed. There seemed to be something wrong in the state of affairs if those who read such patriotic works were under surveillance. But we could not completely grasp the essence of it."[6]

Politics, however, was not entirely all-absorbing for Kemal. He was lonely, socially unsophisticated, and politically unconnected. Pera's adjacent nightlife—akin to locating New York's Greenwich Village and the New Orleans French Quarter three blocks from West Point—was an enormous distraction during his first year of college. Friends, enemies, the secret police, and, later, his best biographers affirmed the complex truth of Kemal's desperate carousing in Pera's taverns and his promiscuous exploits in the brothels.[7]

Though appointed junior sergeant, a prized position among new cadets, Ataturk would describe that first year as lost in a "youthful fantasy" and "youthful reveries." He drank cheap beer in dives with Ali Fethi, his fellow cadet at Monastir, and his class academic ranking plunged.[8] He did meet and become friends with a tall fellow cadet, Ali Fuad Cebesoy. Ali Fuad, the son of a retired Ottoman general, grew up in the capital and introduced Mustafa to his family's prominent circle of civil officials and military elites. Mustafa impressed Ali Fuad's father, Ismail Fazil, and Ali encouraged Mustafa to treat his family's seaside home at Kuzgunjuk as his own. The general became a father figure to Kemal.[9] Ismail Fazil had reformist sympathies, holding what the sultan regarded as independent political views, though the general's influential family provided him with insulation stout enough not only to avoid jail but to serve on the army's general staff.[10] Ali Nazima Pasha, one of Ismail Fazil's friends (he would later become the Ottoman ambassador in Hapsburg Vienna) met Kemal and was struck by his precociousness. Falih Rifki Atay records Ali Nazima as telling Kemal, "You are not going to be an ordinary officer like the rest of us; you are going to change the country's destiny. Don't think I'm flattering you; I see in you the signs of ability and intelligence which great men who are born to rule show even in their youth."[11]

Though he developed an unshakable love for *raki*, Kemal finally began to focus on academics. He displayed a gift for strategy and tactics, and a keen interest in guerrilla warfare. In their third year at the War College, political interest became activism when Kemal and a few friends formed a clandestine society and started a secret political publication.[12]

❖

Kemal graduated as a second lieutenant in 1902. He was eighth in his class of 459 students, so he immediately entered the General Staff College, the institute that prepared the empire's best and brightest for assignment to high-level military staffs. Staff College instructors encouraged his interest in history, with Napoleon's career a compelling subject. Meanwhile, Kemal's political activities continued. The college commandant, Riza Pasha, heard about Mustafa Kemal's clandestine newspaper, but like many educated Ottoman officers, was sympathetic to reform. Riza claimed he would shut down the publication and punish the junior officers, but the commandant never delivered on the threats.[13]

General Staff College studies were more complex than those of the War College. Lieutenant-Colonel Nuri, a respected instructor, taught a tactics course that included lessons in guerrilla warfare. A guerrilla war, Nuri warned his students, is a strategic dilemma: "It is as difficult to suppress it as it is to wage it."[14] Nuri told his class an "uprising can come from inside as well as outside."[15] The idea of an "inside" or domestic partisan war caught Kemal's attention. He outlined a prescient scenario: an insurgent force based in Thrace directing its operations against Constantinople.[16] Kemal's analysis of his staff college scenario is lost to history, but as a war-gamer's what-if, a theoretical concept begging for elaboration, it suggests, in kernel form, the strategy Ataturk would pursue when building the nationalist movement in Anatolia after World War I.

Secret societies far more lethal than Kemal's college conspirators proliferated throughout Rumelia and Anatolia. In August 1903 Slav farmers and villagers in western Macedonia revolted in what became known as the Ilinden Uprising. The revolutionaries proclaimed "Macedonia for Macedonians." Macedonians, however, with Kemal as an example, were ethnically mixed; the revolutionaries favored a Macedonia for Bulgarian Slavs, with Turk and Greek Macedonians viewed as interlopers. A large rebel force assaulted and captured the town of Krusevo (near Monastir) and also launched attacks in eastern Thrace. The Ottomans responded with a series of brutal anti-insurgent operations and by September 1903 had crushed the rebellion. Though poorly coordinated, the uprising demonstrated that well-planned, synchronized attacks, even by irregular forces, might seriously challenge an Ottoman army forced to fight on multiple fronts.

In December 1904 Mustafa Kemal graduated from the college, fifth in a class of forty-three. The top thirteen graduates were promoted to the rank of staff captain, a grade above the rank of captain.[17] While awaiting orders—and hoping for a Macedonia posting because Macedonia's Third Army was the hotbed of reformist military politics—Mustafa remained in Constantinople. He lived in a house in Bayazid with other young officers, including Ali Fuad, where they continued their political discussions. Now, the sultan's police were not sympathetic senior officers but observant overseers devoted to the sultan. A secret agent, posing as a soldier dismissed by the military for political activities, gained the young officers' confidence by asking for help. His ruse worked; the captains gave him a place to sleep but did not mute their opinions.[18] Ismail Hakki, a contributor to the newspaper, was arrested, then Ali Fuad and Kemal. The arrest placed his career and possibly his life in jeopardy.

Ataturk viewed the episode as psychological intimidation; the sultan's routine was to intimidate, then conciliate, with the aim of co-opting opponents. Ataturk described the events to author Falih Rifki Atay in a detached fashion: "Two days after we had decided to help him [the purported soldier] I got a note from him asking me to meet him in a cafe in Bayazid. When I arrived there he had with him an ADC from the palace. Our friend Ismail Hakki was arrested that day, and I the day after....I stayed in solitary confinement for a while, then they took me to the palace...we were accused of illegal publication and organization, and of holding meetings and discussions in our flat....It is probable I owed my freedom to Riza Pasha, the commandant of the college. He sent for me and told me that he knew everything, that he had felt obliged to defend us, but urged us to act more carefully from now on."[19]

No matter how jolly the guards, a stint in an Ottoman jail was a difficult and devilish experience. Kemal feared he would be "banished from the army" and considered fleeing to Western Europe.[20] Just how long Kemal remained in prison is unclear, but he was held at least a week before he was released and reprimanded.

CHAPTER 3

First Assignments, First Revolts

WITH IMPRISONMENT FOR POLITICAL AGITATION ON MUSTAFA KEMAL'S record, an initial tour of duty in Macedonia was highly unlikely. He expected he would be assigned elsewhere, probably to a distant province. This was a professional blow, since Constantinople regarded southeastern Europe, and particularly Macedonia, as the empire's most critical contested territory. Bit by bit the region was slipping from Ottoman control. Following the 1903 Ilinden Uprising, the Murzsteg Reform Program, a peacekeeping operation, placed international observers in Macedonia to direct the Turkish police forces. The great European powers had forced the sultan to accept the plan, which furious Ottomans, particularly those in the Committee for Union and Progress (CUP), saw as yet another affront to Turkish sovereignty and another embarrassing retreat by the feckless Abdulhamid.[1] In Macedonia elite young military officers such as Ismail Enver (who would become minister of war during World War I) confronted the problems posed by the empire's European decline. They also believed Macedonia mattered, and it was there that ambitious young officers polished their professional and political reputations. Kemal viewed duty elsewhere in the empire as either exile or career-stifling punishment.

Ali Fuad faced the same predicament. His father, Ismail Fazil, sympathized, and the retired general pulled some strings to get Fuad and Kemal assigned to the Fifth Army. There appeared to be a wink and nod understanding: with stellar duty reports in all phases of training (cavalry, infantry, and artillery), and no questionable behavior—at least none detected by the secret police—the two might transfer to Macedonia.

The Fifth Army deployed units throughout Ottoman Syria, a demographically and geographically complex area that included parts of early twenty-first century Turkey, Iraq, Syria, Lebanon, Israel, and Palestine (West Bank–Gaza).[2] Ali Fuad received orders for Beirut. The city, Arab yet Levantine and as cosmopolitan in spirit as Pera, had a reputation for fine cafes, beautiful women, and a cooling breeze off the Mediterranean Sea. Kemal's assignment to the Thirtieth Cavalry Regiment placed him in Damascus, at the blistering edge of the Syrian desert. He was the fortunate one of the two, however. For a budding soldier-statesman who understood war was politics by other means, Damascus provided a much more instructive first duty station than libertine Beirut.

Kemal reported to duty in late February 1905. During the empire's halcyon days, spahis had been the flower of the imperial forces, but the Ottoman cavalry had long since declined.[3] After a miserable performance in the Crimean War, the army improved its mounted corps, yet Ottoman cavalry was still regarded as a secondary arm compared to infantry and artillery.

Syrian field duty tested soldiers physically and mentally. Traversing the region's deserts, mountains, dry streambeds, and dismal little towns exhausted—and often broke—infantry and cavalry formations. The terrain itself educated the bones as well as the brain of a staff captain on horseback.

Syria also schooled Kemal in the historical and psychological terrain of human conflict. Ancient antagonisms fed current hostilities throughout Rumelia; he had experienced them as a child and a cadet. In Syria, however, he dealt with their wicked energies in a position which required that he make life and death decisions then enforce them; he was no longer an observer or student. More than a mere shift in perspective, for a career military officer, succeeding in this transition—accepting responsibility and exercising authority in uncertain circumstances—separated leaders from followers.

Damascus also gave Kemal an unfiltered and disturbing look at an Arab *vilayet* (province). Its population was overwhelmingly Muslim, but the cultural, linguistic, and ethnic gap between Arab and Turk was obvious despite centuries of Ottoman rule. Yet, many Arabs proclaimed support for the sultan as the Muslim sovereign protector of the caliphate. By defending the holy sites in the Hejaz, the sultan ensured a degree of respect from them, though many objected to the Turks' Hejaz railway which in 1905 was inching its way toward Medina. The dust and grime staining the Syrian city's streets and squalid quarters did not mask the Arabs' cool resentment. An astute staff captain might conclude shared religion did not guarantee loyalty, not in a medieval, dynastic empire grappling inadequately with the social and economic impact of Europe's revolutions, railways, telephones, and, from America, rumors of powered flight.

Kemal quickly learned that more than a few Ottoman officials and soldiers treated Syria as occupied territory ripe for plunder, not a province populated by fellow believers equal before Allah. Entire units, under the guise of antibandit operations, engaged in theft and extortion in tribal regions. The sultan's corrupt or lackadaisical administrators often failed to pay Ottoman soldiers, giving the Ottoman officers their excuse to tolerate looting.

One version of a story Ataturk told about the situation in Syria involved two other officers with whom he went to the Hamidiye bazaar. "One of them was in command of operations in the Hauran. He was wearing cavalry breeches but on his feet he had slippers. He was a man who took pride in his appearance and Mustafa Kemal asked him to explain this curious get-up. He replied, 'These are the only trousers I have.' This was an officer who would not stoop to stealing." The man wearing civilian shoes with cavalry trousers was Colonel Lufti, the Thirtieth Cavalry Regiment's commander.[4]

Yet, stealing occurred, and Lufti knew about it. Syria's Hauran (Hawran) district was populated by Druse tribes that had a reputation for ferocious resistance to outside interference. Not long after Kemal arrived, a Druse revolt erupted and Fifth Army cavalry units received orders to stop it. Kemal, however, did not receive orders to deploy. He was eager for action, so when he learned of the Hauran operation from a fellow officer, he rode off to speak with the regimental commander, only to be told by Colonel Lufti, "You're still under training.... Besides, you're a staff officer and such jobs are not for you. I assume you'll stay quietly here. You'll still get your pay!"[5] Kemal tried to contact the Fifth Army commander, but the marshal refused to see him, so Kemal and a fellow staff captain in the Twenty-ninth Cavalry Regiment, Mufit Ozdes, rode on their own into the Hauran to join the operation.[6]

What Kemal learned when he got there appalled him. The Ottoman cavalrymen on this expedition were not battling rebels, they were plundering Arab tribes. The theft was organized, after a fashion. The plunderers had subdivided the Hauran into specific zones where individual units looted villages and robbed the locals. Ottoman subjects with sufficient cash, preferably gold, could pay a bribe and avoid robbery. The army in Syria was running a protection racket, not protecting the empire.[7]

A different version of the Hauran story includes an exchange between Kemal and Mufit Ozdes. After Ozdes admitted he had been offered plundered gold, Kemal snapped, "Do you want to be today's man or tomorrow's?" "Tomorrow's, of course," replied Ozdes. "Then you can't take the gold," said Kemal.[8]

Biographer Andrew Mango finds the expedition's tidy details suspicious, calling it a "morality tale" that juxtaposes the future president Kemal the Good against Sultan Abdulhamid the Crooked. The story, however, is firmly embedded in Ataturk's canon. Even if the incident was enhanced for effect, Kemal subsequently displayed in more desperate circumstances the character traits the tale dramatizes. They echo Clausewitz's description of a superior commander's temperament: "A strong character... that will not be unbalanced by the most powerful emotions"—in this case, greed, peer pressure, or fear of reprisal. The Hauran tale describes a passionate man who is not moved by passions of the moment, a man who has "the urge to act rationally at all times" which is key to maintaining a war-fighting commander's "balance."[9]

Mango placed the incident in the context of the Young Turk movement, noting that "revolutionary officers were sincere in their hatred of official corruption; what they wanted was power not money."[10] Corruption had sapped Ottoman will, damaged administration, and weakened the army. Revolutionary organizations, such as the CUP, argued that power in reformist hands, not gold and silver coins on palms, would renew the Ottomans.

❖

Gaining power in the Ottoman Empire, however, would require a political struggle supported by extensive organizational planning. This involved great personal risk. Mango wryly observed, "The Young Turk revolution was a messy affair" in its execution.[11] In its early stages it was a convoluted maze of dicey relationships, covert gambits, and clandestine meetings fueled by burning ambition.

Kemal's odyssey from 1906 through 1908 reflects those of other revolutionary officers. At some time in late 1905,[12] Colonel Lufti introduced Kemal to Mustafa Efendi (later called Mustafa Cantekin), a flesh-and-blood man with the courageous yet tragic background of a minor character in a Dostoevsky or Eric Ambler novel. Mustafa Efendi ran a shop in Damascus's Hamidiye bazaar district. Once a student at Istanbul's Military Medical School, his revolutionary politics had cost him a career in medicine. Arrested in 1900, he spent three years in prison, then was exiled to Syria.[13] In exile he had formed a clandestine organization that became the founding chapter of *Vatan ve Hurriyet Cemiyeti* (Fatherland and Freedom Society),[14] which advocated Ottoman renewal. Kemal joined and "with the excuse of conducting training with various military units" formed new cells in Jerusalem, Beirut, and Jaffa.[15] Ali Fuad joined in Beirut.

Kemal completed his year of cavalry training in early 1906 and was posted to a rifle battalion in Jaffa (Palestine) for his infantry detail. As a student, he had not been certain of the best way to bring change to the empire. Vatan, working through the military, offered a route. Vatan cells in Syria, however, had limited utility. Rumelia, with the Third Army in Monastir and Second Army in Edirne, remained the determinative theater in a strategic political offensive. Ships from Beirut also sailed to Salonika. Kemal saw an opportunity to extend his political organizing operation.

Covert operations in any era require cover and deniability. Kemal's transfer provided both. From December 1905 to October 1906 the rifle battalion conducted operations in the Negev Desert.[16] The desert lay beyond the usual orbits of the sultan's informers. Friends in headquarters can delay, alter, and lose paperwork. Kemal had friends at Fifth Army headquarters. Ahmet Bey, commanding the rifle battalion, was a supporter. Kemal took the boat to Salonika where a friend slipped him through customs. Kemal visited his mother before beginning his rounds.

He had convinced himself that a Macedonian military leader, specifically Sukru Pasha, the senior artillery inspector in Salonika, would support a movement dedicated to saving the empire, so Kemal went to see him. For a soldier absent without leave, approaching Sukru was a brash move, yet Sukru did not call the police. Kemal insisted that he was there because he had written General Sukru a letter and had received an encouraging back-channel reply. However, General Sukru declined to help.[17]

Kemal decided he could not rely on generals. Younger officers and intellectuals were more willing to get involved. He felt that earlier revolutionary initiatives had not succeeded "because they started out without any organization."[18] He had come to Salonika to correct that; he had come to lead.

Several key members of what became the Young Turk movement attended Kemal's Salonika Vatan initiation, including Omer Naci and Hakki Baha, two former War College classmates, and Hursrev Sami and Ismail Mahir. Mehmet Tahir, influential in military and intellectual circles, also participated.[19] The men swore an oath on the Koran and a pistol. The weapon "symbolized their fidelity to the revolution and their intention to resort to arms if need be."[20]

Arguing with generals and swearing oaths on a pistol attracts attention, and Kemal eventually blew his own cover. Army authorities heard rumors Kemal had come to Salonika, arriving with fake travel permits, then flashing health leave orders supplied by a sympathetic doctor. Friends in the Fifth Army alerted Kemal. He departed Salonika, returned to Jaffa, and headed south to his unit in Beersheba in the Negev. False testimony and forged paperwork resolidified the cover story: Kemal had been in the Negev "protecting Ottoman interests in a dispute with the Anglo-Egyptian government over the port of Akaba."[21]

In October 1906 Kemal was reassigned to Damascus for artillery training. On June 20, 1907, he was promoted to adjutant major and then served briefly on the Fifth Army's staff until September 16, 1907, when he received orders posting him to Macedonia.[22]

❖

Macedonia was on the edge of revolution. Kemal's nascent Vatan cell likely inspired others, but if he wanted to lead the movement, his physical presence was crucial. In his absence, Vatan had been absorbed into a larger revolutionary instrument. Now Kemal was a latecomer on the fringe. When he organized the Salonika Vatan cell, the men who eventually emerged as the Young Turk triumvirate (and led the empire into World War I) were already names in Macedonia: Mehmed Talat, the postal service officer; Staff Major Ahmet Cemal; and Adjutant Major Ismail Enver. A Macedonian like Kemal, Enver was a star performer in the Ottoman military system, ranking high in the Staff College class of 1902.

In September 1906, after Kemal dashed back to Syria, Talat formed the Ottoman Freedom Society (OFS). Several members of the Salonika Vatan attended an early OFS meeting in a beer garden, among them Mehmet Tahir and Omer Naci. Cemal and Enver joined Talat. Enver was ordered to start cells in the Third Army headquarters. Other officers organized the Second Army headquarters in Edirne; a young Ismet Inonu joined a Second Army cell in Thrace. The OFS also had an initiation ceremony in which members swore to topple the tyranny of Sultan Abdulhamid and restore the Constitution of 1876, which the sultan had abrogated in 1878. In September 1907, OFS members agreed to join forces with Ottoman exiles and merge the OFS with the CUP. That month Enver was promoted to major. He began leading antibandit operations around Monastir, fighting Albanian, Greek, and Bulgarian gangs. He argued that the CUP should use guerrilla tactics in a revolt. In Salonika, with Talat at the helm, OFS veterans became the "internal center" of the expanded CUP.[23]

Talat, Enver, Cemal—they were the leaders plotting a constitutional revolution. Kemal joined the CUP sometime in February 1908 as a member, not a leader and not in the inner circle of power.[24] H. C. Armstrong's 1933 biography is savagely critical of Kemal, but his portrayal of him as an angry CUP latecomer has the ring of truth: "His criticisms [of CUP leaders] were trenchant and without respect of person. If opposed, he became truculent. He considered the organization of the union and progress casual and inefficient."[25] Armstrong depicts an arrogant Kemal who "had no respect for the leaders. He quarreled with them all: Enver, a slapdash fellow; Jemal, a round-shouldered, swarthy twist-minded oriental; Talat, a post office clerk, a lumbering bear.... His brother officers disliked him as a self-opinionated, sneering fellow. His criticisms were always salty and bitter, with no humor to sweeten them."[26]

In June 1908, the twenty-seven-year-old Kemal was appointed military railway inspector on the link from Salonika to Skopje.[27] Traveling the rail line provided cover for political liaison with CUP cells along the route. According to Ali Fuad, the assignment, despite an implicit level of trust, indicated Kemal was "out of favor" with CUP leaders for his criticisms of "revolutionary policy" both in secret meetings and over drinks in Salonika's cafes.[28] The job sidelined Kemal, who had become an aggressive critic and who was, at the moment, a clear and present nuisance.

Dissatisfaction with the sultan's regime intensified within Macedonian garrisons. In February 1908 a reserve unit refused to deploy to the Hejaz. A commission arrived from Constantinople to investigate. Spies identified revolutionary officers. In the spring of 1908, Great Britain and Russia began discussing new approaches to Macedonian autonomy, which in June led to the Reval Programme. Reval sought but failed to achieve a rapprochement among the Great Powers regarding the Balkans. France welcomed the initiative, Germany and Austria-Hungary did not; what would become World War I's opposing camps clashed diplomatically. Many young Turks believed Reval was hostile to Ottoman interests.[29] The CUP leaders issued a manifesto claiming that only the CUP could bring peace to Macedonia.[30]

In July 1908 the revolt broke out. After discovering a spy had penetrated the CUP network in Resne (now Ohrid), and likely knew of plans for an armed struggle, Major Ahmed Niyazi and soldiers under his command "seized the Resne garrison's arms, ammunition and treasury" and became guerrillas in the backcountry.[31] Within weeks, Enver and Eyup Sabri (Akgol) joined the rebellion.[32]

The initial uprisings were militarily insignificant but politically galvanizing. Beyond the reach of palace guards, the Ottoman army had revolted. Third Army and Second Army CUP members demanded a constitutional restoration. Kemal, inspecting the railroad, had no troops to command, which meant no battlefield glory when glory translated into political power.

Events moved rapidly. On July 7 rebels killed the general whom the sultan had sent to Monastir to end Niyazi's rebellion.[33] In mid-July the sultan ordered military forces in Izmir to sail to Salonika and crush the rebellion. CUP sympathizers, however, had infiltrated the units; when they landed in Salonika they joined the revolt.[34] On July 18, Major General Osman Hidayet, commander of forces in Monastir, was shot.[35] There were no arrests. Towns throughout Macedonia declared for the constitution. The sultan faced the inevitable and on July 23 reinstated the constitution. A new parliamentary assembly would convene.

Despite its lurching start, the rebellion succeeded. The world was alerted by telegraph. Halide Edib Adivar, living in Constantinople, wrote, "The whole empire had caught the fever of ecstasy" which she hoped would lead to a spiritual rebirth.[36] The revolt made Enver, Niyazi, and Sabri "Heroes of Freedom."[37] As for Kemal, at a CUP meeting in Salonika—one he did not attend—the group voted to send him to Tripolitania to explain the policies and goals of the CUP.[38]

It was a lone-wolf assignment.[39] Tripolitania, cut off from the empire by British-controlled Egypt, was divided into two distinct geographic domains: the coastal cities dominated by merchant clans who valued autonomy, and the vast desert of seminomadic tribes whose respect for outside authority varied daily.[40] Arab Muslims in Syria and Arabia were leery of the CUP—after all, Turkey's sultan was the caliph. But Tripolitania was more dangerous.

Anticonstitutional riots occurred in Tripoli and Benghazi. The situation called for self-reliance and creative diplomacy that could reconcile frightened people, religious fanatics, and cynical opportunists. Someone in Salonika must have thought Kemal was up to the task. The committee gave him one thousand Turkish liras in gold for expenses and, when required, for fungible gratuities.[41]

In September 1908, a lieutenant from the Tripoli garrison found Adjutant Major Kemal on the beach, in uniform, where the transport ship's crew had left him. Kemal, turning exile into an opportunity for independent action, was soon living in a general's quarters and meeting local leaders. His presence alone produced results; the honorary British consul in Tripoli, J. Alvarez, was impressed with his "energetic character and resolute temper."[42] Alvarez added, "He is an eloquent and fluent speaker, as I can testify, having heard him expound the principles and objects pursued by his party with remarkable lucidity." Kemal was "applauded by a large audience representative of every class of the population."[43]

Kemal understood the power of oratory. His legendary all-night debates in bars and his speeches as president before the Grand National Assembly demonstrate his verbal aptitude and persuasive intensity, informally and formally. Ataturk later said that in Tripolitania he discovered a number of tribal leaders who "took advantage of the situation by saying that the Caliph's authorities had been greatly diminished with the onset of the Constitutional government....I returned to Salonika after I had re-established the state's authority only after speaking with them in a convincing manner."[44]

If gold helped him calm Tripolitania, in wars at the periphery of power emoluments are an ancient pragmatism. A tribal leader may consider money a payment for services, and recognizing authority a thousand miles away (instead of ignoring it) and providing local security (instead of banditry) are, for a nomad warrior, services. Americans in Afghanistan have encountered the phenomenon. Kemal demonstrated political realism in Tripolitania, leaving "local notables in place, assuring them that constitutional Ottoman government would defend their interests…he was learning how to work with the means available to him. He distinguished between immediate needs and distant goals."[45] In Benghazi the means included surrounding the home of a recalcitrant sheik with soldiers.[46]

Many commentators view Ataturk's Tripolitania assignment as an unfortunate political break or incidental period between the CUP revolt and the 1909 counterrevolution. In North Africa, however, Kemal was not a secondary figure—he was the primary actor. He made decisions, commanded operations, and obtained desired results. In Tripoli and Benghazi, Kemal utilized all of the elements of power (diplomacy, information-intelligence, military, and economic) and achieved what contemporary strategic theorists Qiao Liang and Wang Xiangsui call "consciously combining all of the means available at the time" and thereby "changing the tonality of a war."[47] Kemal accomplished this on a grand scale in the War of Independence. Tripolitania was an instructive precursor, a skill-honing miniature demonstrating an extraordinary talent for comprehensive action.

CHAPTER 4

Counterrevolution, Army of Action, and Its Aftermath

KEMAL RETURNED TO SALONIKA IN JANUARY 1909, ASSIGNED TO THE Third Army's Seventeenth Division as its chief of staff.

The 1908 revolt had shaken the sultan and encouraged reformers, but during Kemal's North African sojourn the CUP had learned that translating the political energy of rebellion into a disciplined, day-to-day government capable of implementing reforms was a formidable project. The Young Turks could conspire, give speeches, and order assassinations, but running bureaucracies, particularly in a culture that venerated age, was not their forte. Moreover, the CUP's base was in Salonika, not Constantinople, and not everyone in the capital was enthusiastic. The sultan and his court certainly were not, nor were hard-line Muslim religious leaders.[1] The CUP, anticipating their objections, had forced the sultan to state that he had restored the constitution in accordance with Koranic law.[2] This did not satisfy the Muslim clerics who saw the revolt as an attack on fundamental Muslim principles of governance.

The CUP attempted to rule through the new parliament and by working with supportive grand viziers and ministers. But conflicts with the sultan's supporters, particularly the politically dogmatic Muslim religious groups, persisted and deepened. In October 1908 Muslim extremists demanded the government return to strict sharia law. Parliament convened in December 1908; the CUP and the sultan maneuvered politically, each seeking advantage as Muslim agitation intensified. In early April 1909 Islamic radicals formed the Ittihad-i Muhammedi (Muhammedan Union), which demanded that Muslims oppose the CUP.

On April 13, 1909,[3] Macedonian units in Constantinople who were previously thought to be pro-CUP rebelled against the new government. Muslim activists had convinced the units' enlisted men that the CUP intended to contravene Islamic law. The rebels imprisoned their officers. The CUP called the action a mutiny, a term that served CUP's political purposes. Whether it was a revolt or mutiny, it was poorly organized. Still, the physical and political threats were real; CUP representatives fled as students and teachers in the capital's religious schools backed the mutineers. The CUP in Salonika decided it must secure Constantinople.[4] CUP officers in the Second and Third Armies quickly organized two composite divisions that began moving on April 15—first by train, then on foot—to Constantinople with orders to quell the mutiny.

Kemal served as chief of staff for Hussein Husnu Pasha who commanded the Salonika division. Lead units arrived on April 19, including a Second Army contingent. The Salonika division closed in on the outskirts of the capital on April 20. Hussein Husnu remained senior commander until April 22, when Third Army commander Mahmud Sevket Pasha arrived and took charge of all CUP units.

The army entered Constantinople on April 23, faced scattered opposition, and by April 24 restored CUP control. Parliament became the Grand National Assembly, echoing the French Revolution's *Assemblée nationale.*[5] With Mehmed Talat as the Assembly's central political figure, it voted to topple Abdulhamid and replace him with his brother, Mehmet Resha, who became Sultan Mehmet V. Kemal's old friend Ali Fethi escorted Abdulhamid into exile in Salonika. The CUP executed eighty individuals as counterrevolutionaries, some of them involved in the revolt, some not.[6]

A military unit's chief of staff coordinates the entire spectrum of staff operations and planning functions, from combat to logistics, transportation, and intelligence. He is a senior adviser and communicator as well as staff director; he translates the commander's strategic and operational intentions into practical planning guidance, then makes certain the plans are produced, understood, and implemented. Though a key position within a military unit, a chief of staff serves the senior commander; he is not leading troops nor is he the public face of the unit; he exerts influence behind the scenes. Several historians note Kemal's peripheral role in the counterrevolution, especially in terms of political and media notoriety. He received very little recognition.[7]

Yet Kemal's talent for quickly identifying critical strategic factors and designing an integrated political and military course of action was effective. Kemal gave the force its name: the Army of Action. Maintaining the entire Ottoman military's loyalty (not just CUP-led forces) was vital to ending the mutiny. What immediate action might help maintain military cohesion throughout the empire? Ataturk later explained how the name—a compelling slogan—succinctly conveyed the political message that the CUP campaign was a fight for Ottoman unity, not a clash of factions: "I came up with the name.... Nobody had understood the meaning at that time. This was the situation. It was necessary to write a declaration that addressed the people of Istanbul. I wrote that declaration. Later, we wrote a second declaration that addressed the [foreign] ambassadors.

We then wondered whose signature would be fitting at the bottom of this declaration. Some friends said the Army of Freedom. When in fact, the entire army was in the position of being the army of freedom. In order to emphasize the position of the forces [i.e., a unified rather than divided military], it was called the freedom army's operation (action) forces."[8]

The name was a piece of practical propaganda, a way of informing the Ottoman military that it was the constitution's bulwark. Kemal realized the CUP needed a name signaling organizational inclusivity and political solidarity. If the name kept potentially rebellious units from joining the mutineers, well and good. He also understood that there was another audience beyond the military. Army bayonets and bullets mattered, but so did the perception of intentions and events. As a nom de guerre, the Army of Action established a psychological context benefiting Kemal's commanders. It was an ancillary act of psychological and information warfare designed to support the main effort. It provided another early career example of Ataturk's comprehensive appreciation of military-political battle space and his quick knack for formulating a course of action to shape it according to his strategic purpose.

Mahmud Sevket received victor's plaudits. In *Scribner's Magazine*, H. G. Dwight, who witnessed the Army of Action's entrance into Constantinople, wrote of Sevket: "Not the least notable among the conquerors of Constantinople will be this grizzled, pale, thin, keen, kind-looking man [Sevket] who, a month before that day, was an unknown corps commander in Salonica…within four days of an equivocal mutiny, he seized the Roumelian railway and put two trains of troops into Chatalja before the reactionaries had time to make their next move. We knew that he had carried out his delicate operations with phenomenal promptness, tact, and strategic ability."[9]

Ismail Enver got glowing headlines too. He raced back from attaché duty in Berlin to lead an attack on mutineers surrounded at Pera's Tashkishla Barracks, which meant the action occurred before the eyes and cameras of international observers a few short steps from a telegraph office. The Tashkishla skirmish was brief but violent. One rifle battalion at the barracks fought with desperation, its soldiers spurred by fear of merciless retribution.[10]

⊕

The telegraph was a modern weapon, one whose power Kemal understood and used. Throughout the drive on the capital, Kemal was seen hustling in and out of telegraph offices, carrying briefcases, passing orders, and editing proclamations.[11] He drafted several statements for his immediate commander, Hussein Husnu. The manifestos issued by the Army of Action were eventually approved by the commanders, which means that they were the product of consultation and discussion, so there are good, common-practice reasons to doubt assertions that Ataturk alone authored the major proclamations. However, throughout the episode Kemal displayed the ability to write clear, concise, and politically astute telegrams under pressure. This skill in the email of its era would reappear when he built the Turkish national movement and rhetorically fenced with the sultan's post–World War I regime.

The proclamations helped create what information-warfare theorists call an "information and perception envelope" for the CUP military thrust into the capital and its subsequent political endeavors. Thanks to the proclamations, Constantinople's urbane natives and foreign visitors anticipated liberation, not subjugation.

The counterrevolution of April 1909 left a lasting mark on the CUP's reformers. To Kemal it demonstrated the ever-present danger of religion-inspired attempts to reestablish a feudal autocracy and stifle the creative vitality modernity demanded. Republican Turkey, under Ataturk's leadership, would base national law on the will of the people as expressed in the Grand National Assembly, not on narrow scriptural interpretations.

In Western Europe, the Peace of Westphalia (1648), which ended the disastrous religious war called the Thirty Years' War, began the process of decoupling religious sects from government. Over time these principles became Western European political practice: government should not intrude on personal faith, and spiritual leaders should counsel political leaders but not exert direct secular control took hold. Christianity, however, began as a faith of the powerless, and political domination was not part of the creed. Islam, in contrast, began with Muhammad's inspired revelation followed by an offensive military explosion. It swept from the Arabian Peninsula west to Spain and east beyond Persia. The Prophet then his successors, the caliphs, combined spiritual authority *and* worldly power. To question the sultan, no matter how impious the man and his regime, could be portrayed as questioning essential tenets of the Muslim faith. Reformers like Kemal knew all too well how Ottoman sultans, with calculated intent, had used this cultural weapon to stir the violent passions of religious militants. When employed, the entire world became a war zone for the sultan-caliph's opponents; they were no longer mere political adversaries or enemies, but heretics scorned by God and subject to mortal reprisal by the faithful, anywhere, at any time.

Kemal returned to duty in the Third Army, and once again became, in the eyes of CUP leaders and senior officers, a nuisance and potential opponent. He was also, however, developing a reputation as a serious thinker dedicated to professionalizing the army. In 1908 Kemal translated into Turkish the acclaimed German infantry expert General Karl von Litzmann's *Instructions for the Conduct of Platoon Combat;* his translation was distributed to Ottoman units and gave him a credential as a student of tactics.[12] Kemal asserted that the Ottoman military must rigorously develop its own talent in order to fully defend imperial interests. When working with foreign advisers, he insisted that Ottoman officers not merely demonstrate their professional skills but exert their authority; observers must not leave with the impression of lack of competence or lack of will.

Kemal led by example. In August 1909, when the eminent German general Baron Colmar von der Goltz arrived for training maneuvers in the Vardar valley near Salonika, Kemal insisted on developing the plans for the exercise. Von der Goltz was highly respected throughout the Ottoman military, having served as an adviser in the 1880s. An acute strategist, Von der Goltz is credited with recommending that the capital, vulnerable to naval attack from European adversaries at that time, be moved from Constantinople to Ankara.[13] Kemal acknowledged the adviser's analysis was valuable, but that "it is even more important that the Turkish staff and commanders should be able to show how their country should be defended."[14] Kemal's plans impressed Von der Goltz—a success for the Third Army staff. Given the adviser's prestige, his appreciation of the sophisticated Turkish-produced plan sent a positive political signal to other foreign instructors and also told perceptive intelligence officers that the Ottoman officer corps was improving.

Kemal's professional advocacy had a contentious twist. Arguing that active participation in politics distracted military officers from their primary duties,[15] he proposed (possibly in a Salonika bar) that military officers resign from the CUP. The proposal aggravated the military leaders, which may have been his purpose since he did not take his own advice. If an ambitious man outside the CUP's inner circle wanted notoriety, he could get it by criticizing the organization's policies publicly. This classical political radical's gambit runs the risk of reprisal but establishes presence. Whether by intent, personality, or a combination of both, Kemal positioned himself as a strong-willed critic offering policy alternatives. He faced physical as well as political threats. Kemal later claimed that he thwarted an assassination attempt in Salonika when an angry CUP member arrived to discuss his criticisms. Kemal placed a revolver on the desk and argued his case. The man was shaken and confessed he had come to kill Kemal.[16]

In 1910 Mahmud Sevket became minister of war. He opposed military membership in the CUP for his own reasons. The Ottoman military's most influential commander until his assassination 1913, he had never joined the CUP and had "in fact challenged the authority of the Committee by trying to forbid officers from belonging to the secret society."[17]

When a series of Albanian tribal-based insurrections erupted in 1910, Sevket returned to Rumelia to lead counterguerrilla operations. He selected Kemal as his chief of staff, who served dutifully even as he criticized what he saw as substandard military skills displayed by senior officers. At one point Kemal declared no one currently serving above the rank of major would remain on active duty if he were in charge.[18]

If Sevket knew of Kemal's intent to sack the entire Ottoman command, he ignored it. In January 1911 Kemal was appointed commander of the Thirty-eighth Infantry Regiment in Salonika, an assignment long overdue. Though abrasive, Kemal's intellect and poise had diplomatic utility, particularly in military-to-military relations. Sevket wanted modern arms "for use against external and internal enemies of the state."[19] In September 1910 Sevket sent Kemal to observe French army maneuvers in Picardy along with the attaché in Paris, Kemal's friend Lieutenant Colonel Ali Fethi.[20]

Airplanes had captured the imagination of European publics as well as the interest of their military officers. The French announced they would test their airplanes as specifically military assets during the autumn field exercises in which 60,000 soldiers would participate. The maneuvers would include the massed fire of thirty batteries of artillery. Nations around the globe, including Japan, a feudal state that had modernized, sent observers.

Kemal, Ali Fethi, and several foreign officers appear in an extraordinary photo taken during the Picardy exercises. In the photo they are listening as French aviation pioneer Colonel Auguste Edouard Hirschauer lectures.[21] The observers display varying degrees of interest—one or two chat, others watch Hirschauer, a pair of men slump, clearly fatigued, another vaguely glances at the photographer. The sharp, razor-straight Kemal, perfectly positioned, looks directly at Colonel Hirschauer and at the camera—he was a man aware of the immediate task as well as the larger audience.

CHAPTER 5

The Turco-Italian War
of 1911–1912

ON SEPTEMBER 13, 1911, ADJUTANT MAJOR KEMAL REPORTED FOR DUTY with the general staff in Constantinople.

A long day's train ride northwest from Constantinople into Europe crossed a multitude of current or imminent battlefields.[1] Despite the Young Turks' proclaimed goal of a multiethnic and politically liberal empire, the Balkans remained a violent mosaic of nationalist intrigues, historical resentments, and ethnic antagonisms. Bulgarian guerrillas plotted revolts around Monastir and Skopje. Greek nationalists in Athens eyed Salonika. Diplomatic sparring among the Great Powers of France, Russia, Great Britain, Germany, and Austria-Hungary, as well an emerging European power, Italy, heightened tensions. European powers great and small made pacts, then swapped threats. Austria-Hungary, after its annexation of Bosnia in October 1908 (an act inflaming Serbia), warned Italy to stay out of Albania. Italy refrained, but Montenegro continued to ship weapons to Albanian rebels. In May 1911 Albanian nationalists, disenchanted by what they considered the Young Turks' unwarranted centralization of state power, demanded that the Ottoman Empire create an expanded, autonomous Albania that included the vilayets of Monastir and Kosovo. Albanian guerrillas launched armed attacks; Ottoman military units responded with counterinsurgency operations; the fierce battles exacted heavy casualties on both sides. Albanian agitation eased when Constantinople offered concessions. However, Serbs, Greeks, and Bulgars viewed Ottoman-Albanian deals with suspicion. Surely these agreements masked a Muslim scheme to create a Greater Albania at the expense of a Greater Greece, Greater Bulgaria, and Greater Serbia.

With Ottoman control of imperial domains near Constantinople visibly tenuous, on September 29, 1911, Italy attacked the empire's even weaker periphery, targeting the North African *vilayet* of Tripoli and igniting the Turco-Italian War.[2] Italian war planners made several strategic and operational calculations. They wagered the Balkan troubles entangling the Ottoman Empire would distract Constantinople. Italy assumed North Africa's political geography worked to its advantage. British-dominated Egypt separated Tripoli (Tripolitania) and Benghazi (Cyrenaica) from the rest of the Ottoman Empire, so the Turks lacked a direct landline of supply to support military operations in the region. In contrast, Italy had a modern navy, built for operations throughout the Mediterranean and, via the Suez Canal, capable of supporting the Italian colonies of Eritrea and Italian Somaliland in east Africa. The Ottoman navy was antiquated. The Italians concluded that they could easily defeat Ottoman naval sorties anywhere in the Mediterranean and that sea dominance would deny the Ottomans the ability to send ground combat reinforcements rapidly, if at all. Moreover, Italian naval gunfire provided a tactical firepower advantage should Turkish forces attempt to mass against Italian forces near the coastline.

For three decades Italy had coveted Ottoman possessions in North Africa and the Aegean. Status in Europe meant strong military forces, an industrial economy, and foreign colonies. Italy, which did not unify until 1861, came late to the colonial competition, though its new imperial aspirations revived old history. Despite centuries of Arab and then Turkish dominance, the classical Roman provincial designations of Tripolitania and Cyrenaica lingered as popular names for the region. Genoa had once controlled the Aegean islands of Lesbos, Chios, and Samos; Venice once held Cyprus. Now Italians would reclaim their lands.[3] Italian strategy did not rely solely on the sword. Since 1900 Italy had pursued "peaceful penetration" using soft economic and diplomatic power. At the government's behest, the Banco di Roma invested throughout Tripolitania, building "grain elevators, electrical works, factories…gradually securing a kind of mortgage on the province that might, if necessary, provide an opportunity for armed intervention."[4] The Ottomans tried to stymie these efforts. When Constantinople restricted bank activities, however, Italy declared the Ottoman reaction criminal. This grievance incited Italian nationalist passions.

By 1911 Italian diplomats "had secured the tacit agreement of Britain, France, and Russia and at least neutrality on the part of Germany and Austria" for expansion into Tripolitania.[5] The situation appeared favorable. That year Constantinople, eyeing the Balkans' fragile balance, reinforced its units fighting Yemeni rebels with part of its North African garrison, the Forty-second Infantry Division.[6] In May 1911 French troops occupied Fez, the capital of Morocco, sparking the Second Moroccan Crisis. Germany objected and sent a cruiser; Great Britain and Russia backed France; Germany backed down, withdrawing its warship. The crisis, called the Agadir Incident, strained Great Power relations.[7] It isolated Germany and fueled German suspicions of France. The Moroccan naval embarrassment influenced Berlin's decision to mobilize three years later, in 1914, after the assassination of Austria's Archduke Franz Ferdinand in Bosnia. Germany's navy could be trumped, but not its army. Germany would not back down again. Sixteen million people would die in World War I.

In the heady summer months of 1911, however, Italy's ambitious leaders saw opportunity. Fevered minds in Rome, dreaming of "Tripolitania Bella,"[8] concluded that another Great Power might intervene in North Africa if Italian forces failed to act swiftly and decisively.[9]

❖

The Turco-Italian War was an asymmetric war in an impoverished backwater. It was the first in an explosive chain of three wars involving the Ottomans, each a precursor of World War I, the Great War. Kemal was a witness to, participant in, and student of all three.

Italian military planners had noticed France's 1910 Picardy maneuvers. The Turco-Italian War was the world's first air war, and the Italians employed aircraft in reconnaissance and attack operations. Dirigibles dropped bombs—a forerunner of World War I's zeppelin attacks on London. Pilots in Bleriot XI monoplanes lobbed hand grenades at camel-borne Arab auxiliaries who replied with rifles. At that early stage, close air support was an awkward and intimate encounter.

The Turco-Italian War offered other bloody glimpses of the future. As the Italian invasion bogged down in trenches outside Tripoli, Tobruk, and Derna, the Italians sought a war-altering strategic coup in another theater. They took the Dodecanese Islands off southwestern Anatolia; they conducted naval probes of the Dardanelles and their warships shelled other Ottoman possessions in the eastern Mediterranean and Red Sea. These Italian naval and amphibious operations, like the 1915 Allies' assault on Gallipoli, were ventures bred by the hope of escaping an entrenched war of attrition.[10]

What Italy confronted in 1911, the Greeks would face as Kemal organized resistance in Anatolia. Italian forces could not close Ottoman supply routes as the Turkish military received supplies across allegedly neutral borders. France would face similar limitations and frustrations in Algeria, the United States in Vietnam, and Russia in Afghanistan. The Italians would not attack sanctuaries in British-controlled Egypt and French-controlled Tunisia, any more than the United States would attack southern China when it served as a supply dump for North Vietnam. The big question for the Turks was the loyalty of Arab and Berber tribes. They distrusted Constantinople, with reason: corrupt colonial administrators cheated them. The Turks' North African colonies suffered from misgovernance and malign neglect. To maintain tribal loyalty, the sultan appealed to Muslim sympathies and declared jihad—but the Ottomans also paid tribesmen with cash.[11]

Italy's conventional forces suddenly faced dispersed guerrilla formations led by capable Ottoman officers schooled in tribal politics and insurgent operations. Kemal exhibited both skill sets in an exemplary fashion during the Tobruk operations at Nadura Hill and at Derna, west of Tobruk.

❖

Anticipating an Italian invasion, Constantinople dispatched the freighter *Derne* to Tripoli with a cargo that included 12,000 rifles and ammunition. The *Derne* docked in Tripoli on September 25, 1911. The next day the Italian navy blockaded Tripolitania from the Egyptian to Tunisian borders to thwart future Ottoman resupply ships. On September 28 Rome demanded that Constantinople allow Italian troops to land in Tripoli to protect Italian citizens. It was a sham demand, for a day later Italy declared war. An hour after the declaration Italian destroyers sank two Turkish patrol boats in the Adriatic Sea between the island of Corfu and port of Preveza.[12] Italy then ordered the surrender of Tripoli. When the

Turks refused, on October 3 Italian warships began bombarding the city. The Tripoli garrison, commanded by Colonel Neset, withdrew inland, abandoning much of its artillery but taking its stocks of rifles and cartridges for distribution to desert tribes. Italian soldiers landed in Tripoli on October 5. A small Italian landing force had taken Tobruk the day before. Derna fell on October 16, and Benghazi, October 20.[13]

The Italian invasion force (approximately 22,500 troops, 6,000 horses and mules, 800 wagons, 30 guns, and 4 airplanes) vastly outmatched Ottoman conventional forces. In Tripoli the Ottoman army deployed some 3,000 soldiers, formed as three battalions of infantry (700 men each), with an additional 210 sharpshooters, 279 cavalrymen, and the rest, artillery troops. In Benghazi the Ottomans had 800 infantrymen, 150 cavalrymen, and 200 artillerymen.[14] Following the rapid occupation of the port cities, the Italian invasion stalled. At Tripoli Colonel Neset's forces simply retreated beyond naval gun range, establishing division headquarters 80 kilometers to the south in Garyan. The front line shifted away from the easy coast and into the difficult desert.

CUP officers committed to revitalizing the empire scrambled to get into North Africa. The empire, under its CUP-led government, would not suffer another loss and indignity. Major Ismail Enver, serving as military attaché in Berlin, went to Salonika and urged the CUP to wage a guerrilla conflict.[15] Bitter personal experience had shown Turkish officers that professional soldiers leading committed partisans could torment superior conventional forces; Serbian, Greek, and Bulgarian officers had led and advised their fierce ethnic irregulars in Ottoman Rumelia. Enver thought Italy's generals should confront the wicked combination of Turkish elite combat officers and desert tribal fighters.[16]

Enver then left for Cyrenaica. Ali Fethi, still in France, left Marseilles on a boat for Tunis. Once there, he slipped across the border and made contact with the Tripoli garrison in the desert. Kemal, having personal knowledge of Arab tribal fighters and direct experience in Tripolitania, volunteered for duty in Africa.

The minister of war, however, would not fully sanction the Tripolitania operation. Instead, he officially described the officers as "volunteers," a term that provided thin but useful diplomatic deniability.[17] Kemal, an old hand at clandestine travel, took passage on a Russian ship, disguised as a journalist named Sherif.[18] He sailed from Constantinople for Alexandria on October 15.

Eight days later, Arab and Berber tribesmen collaborating with Turkish forces attacked Italian forces entrenched outside of Tripoli. The tribal warriors suffered heavy losses but killed almost 500 Italian soldiers.[19] British journalist Ernest N. Bennett visited Ottoman forces in Tripolitania from late 1911 through January 1912 and saw the Ottoman strategy in action. At some point Italy risked a "bad reverse in the desert," he wrote. Over time, a "protracted campaign would drain Italian military and economic resources, opening "the possibility of a violent change in popular feeling [in Italy] if the war is unduly prolonged without any salient results." Bennett identified Ottoman vulnerabilities, including questionable Arab loyalty: "One of the most serious handicaps on the Ottoman side is the existence of internal dissensions. If the Turks will only lay aside political intrigues and disagreements at home and present a united front to the enemy" then Italy might be defeated.[20]

The resistance in October and November startled Rome. The Italians understood they were short of troops and a gradual escalation began. Before 1911 was over another 55,000 soldiers arrived, with 8,300 mules, 1,300 wagons and carts, 84 large artillery pieces, and 42 mountain guns.[21]

On October 10, 1911, Minister of War Sevket issued strategic guidance for North Africa. Guidance is one way to describe it; another would be wishful thinking. "We face many difficulties....Our soldiers' honor requires that we must accept the burden and begin combat operations. You are to remain in Tripoli until the last Ottoman soldier is alive. I give this command to you. The honor of Muslims and Ottomans is in your hands." Sevket added that money and supplies would be sent "through Tunisia and Egypt."[22]

Kemal reached Alexandria in late October. In a letter written in May 1912 to his friend Kerim Bey, he indicated he tried to leave the city on November 2, 1911. "I came from Istanbul with Naci Hakki [Omer Naci] and Yakup Cemil. We had only 300 lira among us. We reached Alexandria where I became sick. I had to remain in Egypt for 15 days in the hospital in Alexandria." While there, he linked up with two old friends and fellow officers, Nuri Conker and Fuat Bulca. The trio made plans to cross the Egyptian border. Security, however, was tight, and they were detained as they crossed the Egyptian border.[23]

Biographer Patrick Kinross describes the detention as an arrest deflected by Kemal's aggressive tactics. Kemal disguised himself as an Arab traveler; Conker and Bulca claimed they were law students. Three other infiltrators linked up with them in Egypt—an Ottoman army gunner, an Arab interpreter, and an Egyptian guide. At the end of the Egyptian rail line running west from Alexandria, an Egyptian security officer announced he had orders to arrest five Turkish military officers. Kemal, aware that their disguises were useless, "revealed their identity and harangued the Egyptian with an appeal to his religious sentiments." The Egyptian agreed to a deal. Kemal, Conker, and Bulca could proceed, but one man had to remain in custody, pending further orders. The "next day all but the Turkish gunner were released." Kemal and his party continued west with the men on horseback and the equipment on camels. They encountered a British-Egyptian patrol. Kemal told the British officers he and his men would fire on them if they did not withdraw. The British insisted the Turks were in Egyptian territory but "laughed...shrugged their shoulders, and let them go."[24] The rest of the trip went without incident and the group joined Ottoman forces in the Tobruk area December 9.

❖

Despite the Italian naval blockade, an impressive collection of Ottoman military talent had assembled in North Africa, including Mustfa Kemal, Ismail Enver, Ali Fethi Okyar, Fuat Bulca, Nuri Conker, and Ali Cetinkaya.[25] Kemal was definitely overshadowed politically and in the media spotlight. Enver had established himself in Benghazi. Despite the presence of an Ottoman general, Ethem Pasha, at Tobruk, Enver assumed military, political, and media command of the Cyrenaica region. Enver was, after all, an international figure and the big name in the group, though outside Tripoli the cosmopolitan Ali Fethi dazzled reporters with his courage and charisma. In the North African war zone Kemal's CUP rival and his trusted compatriot were recognizable characters: Enver the dashing Young Turk forever promoting himself, Ali Fethi the urbane Ottoman gentleman. Fethi was, as one writer put it, "a tall, fair Albanian of about thirty-five, with a quiet, cultured manner and an unfailing courtesy—is reputed to be the ablest [Ottoman officer] of all.... He is anything but robust physically; yet he has volunteered to exchange the luxuries of Paris for the hardships of the wilderness, and he has been roughing it like one of the most primitive peasants for three months."[26]

❖

In his May 1912 letter to Kerim Bey, Kemal mentioned that once he reached Tobruk, he took the lead in a successful combat action involving Senussi tribal warriors.

Kemal was referring to the Battle of Nadura Hill. Fought on December 22, 1911, it was a battle of limited success but exemplary for a war in which the Ottomans gambled that limited tactical successes would eventually erode Italian will.

Nadura Hill is a rugged knoll a little more than two kilometers south of Tobruk's long harbor. A peninsula extending east from the mainland forms the harbor; in 1911 the city of Tobruk occupied the closed crook of the peninsula, at the harbor's western end. Three months after Tobruk's occupation the Italians had advanced only as far as Nadura Hill, which demonstrated their operational limitations and strategic dilemma. Their inadequate supply and transport system could barely handle forays along the coastal escarpment; desert sand and heat killed the wagon mules that snipers and disease did not. Unsupported cavalry columns penetrating the interior became targets of opportunity, harassed by nomads on faster camels and stouter horses, or ambushed by sharpshooters. Nascent airpower provided intermittent observation, but its firepower ranged from the negligible to the comically entertaining. Italian ground forces hugged the coast, relying on their naval guns for protection.

Kemal spent his first days in the Tobruk area conducting reconnaissance and meeting with the Senussi sheiks and their leader, Sheik Muberra. Italian activities attracted his attention on and around Nadura Hill, where he detected an Italian buildup. "Kemal told the sheiks the Ottoman forces should attack before the Italians reinforced and improved the position. Since the Arab warriors had received ammunition following their training (with the new weapons), Kemal said they should attack the enemy position."[27]

Familiarity with weapons is one skill, but unit battle drill is much more complex; creating combat units takes time, training, and discipline. As Chinese strategist Sun Tzu argued in *The Art of War* (Book 3, Planning an Offense), "By perceiving the enemy and perceiving ourselves (yourself), there will be no unforeseen risk in any battle."[28] Perceiving yourself includes knowing your own troops' capabilities. Kemal understood the Senussi fighters under his command. They were experienced desert warriors, not soldiers schooled in conventional battle drill. He had to work with what he had, so Kemal advised the Senussi tribal leaders, organized their forces, and planned operations.[29] The sheiks knew their warriors were not schooled in modern conventional warfare with artillery preparations and coordinated infantry assaults. Their warriors had experience in the tactics of the raid—deception, infiltration, close attacks with firearms and knives. The Senussi sheiks told Kemal that they would prefer to use their own methods and tactics. Kemal agreed and he forwarded this recommendation to Ethem Pasha, the Ottoman commander at Tobruk, who approved Kemal's decision. Ethem Pasha sent twelve local Cretan Turk volunteer soldiers—Turks who had moved to Tripolitania from Crete to avoid Greek rule—to reinforce Sheik Muberra's assault.

On the evening of December 21 Sheik Muberra took 120 tribesmen and began moving toward enemy lines on Nadura Hill, three kilometers north of the Ottoman positions. Just before dawn on December 22 they launched a series of assaults, catching the Italians by surprise. The Italian infantry replied with erratic and uncoordinated rifle and machine gun fire. They had not installed field artillery in the new trenches. In the next two hours, the tribesmen then completely surrounded the hill and its fortifications, indicating Sheik Muberra's assault group received reinforcements. The Italians who were not surrounded fled toward Tobruk, abandoning three machine guns and other equipment.[30]

Sheik Muberra's tribesmen began destroying enemy fortifications. However, Italian reinforcements arrived and counterattacked, catching part of the Arab force exposed on the far slope of the hill. Sheik Muberra received reinforcements who immediately entered the fight and helped smash the counterattack. The battle ended early in the afternoon with the Senussi fighters in full control of the position. The tribesmen did not celebrate their victory: in the chaos following the counterattack, a bullet struck Sheik Muberra in his forehead; he fell and died on the slope. Nadura Hill had cost the Senussi battle chief his life.

Kemal, from a position west of Nadura Hill, returned to the sector to oversee postcombat operations and collect the arms and ammunition the fleeing Italians left on the battlefield. "The Turks, however, never took advantage of the victory. Ultimately the Italians returned, rebuilt the Nadura fortifications and this time added numerous artillery pieces to the defense."[31]

Occupying the position ran grave risks. The Ottoman defense had to be flexible, holding the Italians near the coast without engaging in battle where the Italian artillery advantage would deal a decisive defeat. In mid-December at least four Italian capital ships were stationed at Tobruk or patrolled nearby waters: *Vittorio-Emanuele, Pisa, Etna,* and *Etruria.*[32] The ships had impressive batteries of twelve-, ten-, and eight-inch guns. Ottoman forces occupying Nadura Hill would have faced these naval guns as well as Italian army field artillery. Exposing Ottoman forces to heavy naval guns by attempting to hold a fixed, observed position within their range violated common sense. Retrieving abandoned weapons and supplies and then returning to the desert was savvy. They retreated beyond gun range, let the Italians reoccupy a position, then struck again. For their part, Italian commanders were reluctant to employ naval firepower when Italian infantry and Ottoman raiders mixed in close combat; in this situation, especially at night, huge rounds were highly likely to indiscriminately kill Italian soldiers.[33]

Kemal would encounter modern naval cannon and this defensive dilemma again—at Gallipoli.

⬥

Kemal utilized psychological and information warfare techniques. At Derna he insisted that his officers subscribe to journals and papers from around the globe. He wanted his officers to know the world was watching and that their actions shaped opinions. Kemal understood the power of words, images, symbols, and symbolic behavior, and insisted his officers dress well. Personal carriage, discipline, and intellectual preparation affected perceptions. At the tactical level it impressed the men under their command; the sophisticated, confident presentation also impressed diplomats and reporters and symbolized Ottoman military professionalism. Linking the immediate tactical situation to larger, strategic military and diplomatic goals, he did not want his officers "to give the impression they were average men."[34]

Kemal's insistence on sharp personal appearance and discipline, even in harsh desert conditions, carried over to Kemalist politics in republican Turkey. In Cyrenaica, Kemal had "stressed cleanliness, discipline, order and drill on and off the battlefield, as well as unconventional initiatives in the fighting itself; the importance of outward appearance and the belief that symbols can influence thought and behavior became characteristics of Kemalist Turkey."[35] Kemal emphasized the details that make the difference in tactical and operational combat. Turkish historian Hamdi Ertuna observes that "Mustafa was very thorough in his reconnaissance procedures and personally observed everything. He himself controlled his military scouts in reconnaissance operations. He also paid detailed attention to supplies, to the point of making sure his men's canteens were full before they started."[36]

Military commanders know the immense value of personal reconnaissance at the front, but the commander cannot be everywhere. A commander must receive accurate information. Kemal's July 22, 1912, order to his officers and men at Derna is instructive.

> Reports regarding the Ottoman-Italian war must rely on information gathered by members of this force.
>
> All reports should include Date, Conditions, Actual Forces, the plans and orders of top commanders, the operation involved, and the results of those operations. Every participating soldier should report losses objectively (no lies). Prepared reports should reflect real battlefield conditions. All soldiers should remain loyal to truth and humanity. Reports should be forwarded within a month.
>
> Mustafa Kemal, Commander Derna[37]

No lies. Accurate reports were essential to improving training and tactics and winning the next battle. Kemal would not let his men—Turk, Arab, or Berber—tell him what they thought he wanted to hear. He confronted head-on institutional and cultural inclinations to exaggerate success or deny failure. He created new inclinations by imposing discipline, leading by example, and holding individuals accountable.

Kemal would later observe, "Wars are made by people. An army's value is determined by the value of its officers. The commander is a person who has creative powers."[38]

❖

Derna, west of Tobruk, saw some of the campaign's most bitter battles.

"When someone talks about Derna," Hamdi Ertuna writes in his study of the Turco-Italian War, "it is impossible not to remember Mustafa Kemal, for it can be said that it was there, at Derna, Kemal's commander's skills fully revealed themselves for the first time....For Italians their defense of Derna holds some of the worst historical memories."[39]

In February 1912 Italy deployed fifteen to sixteen thousand troops around Derna. Italian forces included five infantry regiments (each with three battalions and supporting machine gun detachments), seven separate battalions (three of them elite alpine infantry units), a 120mm field artillery battalion, two mountain artillery battalions, a naval artillery unit, and a wireless telegraph communications group. Turkish forces consisted of 8 officers leading 7,742 Arab fighters, 98 Turkish infantrymen, 105 Turkish volunteers, 6 cavalrymen, 17 artillerymen, 3 volunteer artillerymen, and 15 men in machine gun detachments. Another 110 militia men were available if needed. The Turkish troops and volunteers were flagged as a battalion of the 124th Infantry Regiment, Forty-second Infantry Division,[40] while an additional 8,000 Arab fighters raised the battlefield rifle strength to that of a division. This necessitated organizational improvisation. In his May

1912 letter to Kerim Bey, Kemal wrote that the Ottomans organized the Derna forces as one division but fought as two wings: "Our forces at Derna were divided by a valley. I was initially with the western forces. Then we made Nuri [Conker] commander of that wing and I fought as east wing commander." The terrain directly influenced this decision. The deep and arid valley running south from Derna creates two different operational areas with Derna located at the seaward end. At Sidi Abdullah was a graveyard, the valley's key position, and two kilometers from there the Italians initially entrenched. Later they fortified a position approximately 800 meters southwest of the graveyard—within machine gun range. After the Italians dug in near Sidi Abdullah, the Ottomans concluded that "the Italians did not have the courage to go any further into the interior, therefore they built many bunkers." Ertuna's Italian order of battle includes five infantry regiments, and three separate Alpine battalions. Ottoman intelligence believed the troop buildup would continue.[41]

The Derna forces continually probed and harassed the Italians. Ertuna says the Derna force "did not let the enemy rest. Every night. At different hours each night a force of 15 or more men attacked the Italians. After Kemal's arrival at Derna in January, he had made detailed plans for some of these harassment attacks.[42] An earlier night attack on January 16, 1912, however, had not gone well. Kemal had inspected the Arab forces and discovered they were ill prepared for battle. Suspecting that they were reluctant to fight, he spoke to them and insisted that the operation was important. The Arab sheiks demurred. They found fault with the orders; they argued. Finally, the sheiks agreed to launch the raid. They gathered three or four dozen men, with only fifteen rifles among them. A night raid on a trench without a rifle is not necessarily a mistake; knives in the hands of men who know how to use them are effective close-quarters weapons. But Kemal reported that this particular night raid failed to produce positive results. Still, the incessant raids convinced the Italians they did not have enough troops at Derna.

In a subsequent attack, likely on January 17, Kemal was ambushed and suffered a wound to his left eye.[43]

On March 3, 1912, a small Ottoman force of seventy men carefully probed Sidi Abdullah from the west, getting close enough to surprise the Italians occupying forward defensive positions. The startled Italians fled those forward positions while their artillery responded quickly with protective fire. Before noon the battle intensified as Turkish artillery started shelling the Italians. Observers reported the artillery scored several direct hits on key positions. Suddenly a large Ottoman infantry force attacked Sidi Abdullah from the south. The Ottomans threw everyone available in the southern sector into the assault, even couriers and medical personnel. The hard-pressed Italians responded with artillery fire and additional infantry reinforcements.[44] When the Italians were completely engaged, Kemal's wing attacked the Italian left flank, pouring into the valley from the east. The Italians failed to hold their positions and began to retreat from the area in the early evening. The Turkish forces then proceeded to take all of the Italian trenches, counting the enemy losses at 200 dead and retrieving 60 rifles. "Based on the uniform patches Ottoman fighters found on the Italian dead, the Italians had four battalions in the entrenched position. The Ottomans lost 63 dead and 168 wounded. This attack discouraged the Italians and they did not attack again for quite some time."[45] Nuri Conker wrote that in the March 3 battle "we forced the Italians to evacuate their recent gain of five kilometers (in the area) and retreat back to their old positions." He recalled that Ottoman forces had four mountain artillery pieces in support and "five to six hundred" Arab volunteers, most of the Arabs attacking "without ammunition." He added, "We captured much loot and many prisoners."[46]

The tactical victory dealt the Italians a psychological defeat. Despite their advantage in soldiers and firepower, they chose to wait and not attack. In the Ottomans' estimation, the longer the Italian invader waited, the more discouraged they would become, and the day of their withdrawal would be that much closer.

Kemal officially became the commander of the Derna front on March 6.[47] In May he would write his friend Kerim, "We now have other divisions two to three days distance from us [in Derna]. Our forces in Benghazi [Cyrenaica] are very determined and the enemy continues to prepare defense positions."[48]

✦

Ottoman units controlled the desert, but they lacked the power to drive the Italians into the sea. The Ottomans sought to exhaust Italy strategically in both mind and spirit. Even minimal military pressure preserved political options. Kemal made certain the Italian forces facing him at Derna would confront relentless psychological pressure. Every night at different hours raiding parties probed Italian positions, sniped at Italian observation posts, and occasionally launched local attacks. Kemal provided his raiders with very detailed tactical plans.[49]

The Italians could not destroy the Ottoman forces by depriving them of sustenance and military support. Money and Arab smugglers had created a crude supply line capable of providing sufficient materiel to support relentless small-scale raids and occasional conventional forays like the attack on Sidi Abdullah. Military attachés, like Commodore Beehler, had detailed knowledge of the ad hoc supply system through which officers and men, weapons and ammunition, and all kinds of supplies flowed across the porous Egyptian and Tunisian frontiers.[50]

The Italians' domestic political clock ticked. Ignoring the Great Powers who had warned them to avoid military action in the Adriatic and Aegean, in 1912 the Italians invaded the Dodecanese Islands. They launched their own probes, shelling Dardanelles' fortifications, threatening Rumelia's and Anatolia's coasts. These actions had two goals: to preserve domestic support and to create diplomatic bargaining chips. But they also had an ironic consequence. Military observers at the time noted that Turkish coastal guns were ineffective, and this became the conventional wisdom regarding the Dardanelles' shore defenses.[51] In late 1914 Winston Churchill, to his everlasting regret, would also accept it as received truth.

Two competing strategic clocks, the one in the North African desert and the one in the Balkans, also continued to tick. In 1912 the Balkan League of Serbia, Bulgaria, Greece, and Montenegro was formed. The league was brittle; Serbia disliked Bulgaria; Bulgaria disliked Serbia and wanted to keep Greece from claiming Macedonia, especially Salonika. Greece, however, had a navy. The looming Italian-Ottoman peace would permit the transfer of Ottoman troops from Beirut and Izmir to Salonika. Greek warships could prevent seaborne reinforcement. And so Bulgaria warily accepted Greece as an ally.

Ottoman and Italian diplomats met in Switzerland to discuss a peace treaty. The North African clock slowed down; the Balkan clock ticked faster. In September 1912, one year after the Italian invasion of Tripolitania, Bulgarian forces began mobilizing. As the Swiss negotiations progressed, Ottoman attacks on the Italian forces declined. Except in Derna.

On October 8, 1912, Montenegro attacked Ottoman Albania, igniting the First Balkan War. The Ottoman war with Italy quickly ended. The defeated Ottomans ceded Tripolitania to the Italians; with their prize in hand, the delighted Italians agreed to give the Turks a small face-saving compensation. Italy would return the Dodecanese Islands to the Ottomans. As the Greeks, Bulgars, and Serbs advanced in Rumelia, however, the double-dealing Italians broke the brand-new treaty. Rome would keep the Aegean island chain after all, and the Turks, their armies now pressed against the gates of Constantinople, could do absolutely nothing about it.

CHAPTER 6

The Balkan Wars

"How could you surrender that beautiful Salonika to the enemy?"

—Mustafa Kemal

THE WAR BEGAN WITH A SURGE. THE BALKAN LEAGUE ARMIES STRUCK quickly, crippling then surrounding Ottoman forces in Macedonia while smashing Ottoman resistance in eastern Thrace.

Boots, horses, and horse-drawn wagons were the primary means of military movement (with an occasional operational assist from railroads), yet combat proceeded at a near-blitzkrieg pace. The brunt of the fighting occurred in October and November 1912, beginning with the October 8 Montenegrin attack on the Albanian fortress of Scutari. Serbs advanced west and south, scattering units in Macedonia. The Serbs seized Kumanova on October 24, then, in mid-November, Monastir. On November 8, through a combination of hard combat, speedy pursuit, and sly diplomatic coup, the Greek Army of Thessaly took Kemal's beautiful Salonika. This Greek coup enraged the Bulgarian forces racing toward the Aegean port from the north. The Bulgarians coveted Salonika and the canny Greeks had beaten them to it.

In Thrace the Bulgarians defeated the Ottomans in an enormous battle at Kirkkilise, surrounded Edirne, and, until they slammed into the Catalca Lines (fortifications that ran north to south along the Catalca ridgeline) in mid-November, seemed likely to storm Constantinople. Shattered Ottoman forces regrouped in Catalca's fortifications west of the capital and stopped the series of bitter attacks launched by the Bulgarian army.

On December 3 Bulgaria, Serbia, Montenegro, and the Ottoman Empire agreed to an armistice. The Balkan League's forces were exhausted; the reeling Ottomans needed time to reinforce. This first armistice temporarily halted major combat but did not cool the antagonists' passions. Bulgarian forces continued to advance south and southwest. On December 12 the Bulgarians encountered Ottoman gendarmes on the outskirts of the Marmara seaport of Sarkoy. They skirmished for ten days until local commanders established a ceasefire. This advance to Sarkoy effectively split the Ottoman First Army and cut off land communication routes with the Gallipoli Peninsula.

Greece did not accept the December 1912 ceasefire. In January 1913 Greek forces surrounded the Ottoman fortress city of Yanya in Epirus. That month, the assassination of Ottoman war minister Nazim Pasha and a coup d'état led by Ismail Enver—who favored renewed war and the relief of Edirne's surrounded garrison—shook the empire. Kemal and Ali Fethi, both serving with units in Gallipoli, bitterly opposed the violent and murderous coup, which would sow deep distrust in the new regime and might harm the reputation of the military.

The first armistice expired February 3, 1913, and the war reignited. The Bulgarians snatched Sarkoy on February 4. The Ottomans attempted an ill-fated counterstroke, an attack at Boyalir on the Gallipoli Peninsula paired with an amphibious assault on Sarkoy; the operations failed.

Greek besiegers took Yanya's great fortress on March 6, 1913, then pushed further north into Albania. Surrounded Edirne surrendered to Bulgaria on March 24. Other unsupplied Turkish garrisons on scattered Aegean islands began capitulating. The noose of the Greek navy had strangled and starved them. Constantinople could do nothing to save its isolated soldiers. Though Montenegro fought until April 23, on April 15 the rest of the Balkan League and the Ottoman Empire accepted a general armistice, the Second Armistice. The Treaty of London, signed May 30, 1913, ended the war. The treaty's terms angered Bulgaria. Just one month later, on June 29, 1913, the Second Balkan War erupted when Bulgaria attacked its former allies, Serbia and Greece.[1]

❖

Kemal left North Africa and raced to Constantinople, reaching the city in early November 1912. The surrender of Salonika—without a shot—had outraged him. He knew his mother and sister had fled, as had thousands of ethnic Turks. Fleeing western Thrace and avoiding Greek and Bulgarian forces was dangerous and difficult. Winter had arrived with its cold, soaking rain. Miserable bands of refugees filtered into the capital.[2] First they had fled their homes in Macedonia and Thrace; now they fled the typhus- and cholera-ravaged hasty refugee camps erected outside the city. Wounded soldiers in need of medicine packed Constantinople's mosques, hospitals, and homes. Everyone needed food, warmth, and a roof.[3]

The bloody standoff at nearby Catalca continued. Residents of Constantinople and glum soldiers defending the city could hear the distant rumble of heavy cannon fire. Kemal joined several fellow officers in a Constantinople cafe and, after a painful silence, he exclaimed, "How could you do this? How could you surrender that beautiful Salonika to the enemy? How could you sell it so cheaply?"[4]

Profoundly shaken by the news Salonika had fallen, Kemal would later tell Nuri Conker its loss inflicted a terrible wound, for it meant "my mother, my sister, all my relatives and relations, had been delivered to the enemy."[5] But he learned his immediate family and a few distant relatives had in fact escaped to Constantinople. When Kemal finally located them, he rented a house in Pera for his mother, Zubeyde; his sister, Makbule; Zubeyde's husband, Ragip; and two of Ragip's nieces, Fikriye and Julide.

✛

How had the Turks lost the First Balkan War?

The title of Edward J. Erickson's study of the Balkan Wars provides a crisp military assessment of the Ottoman failure: *Defeat in Detail*. The phrase "defeat in detail" is the classic term for defeating an enemy who employs forces piecemeal. When combat power is fragmented rather than used in a powerful, synergistic mass, the fragments can be engaged and destroyed separately. A smaller force massing combat power against a larger force so ill-used or ill-deployed effectively becomes the stronger one. Ottoman forces in Rumelia tried to defend every *vilayet*, no matter how untenable; as a result they defended next to nothing. Their only success was along the Catalca Lines outside the capital, where they concentrated and protected their forces. Had they lost the Catalca fortifications, the Turks might have lost Constantinople. As Erickson observes, "Although the Turks enjoyed an apparent margin of numerical superiority, geography forced them to split their forces into smaller groups to oppose their individual enemies."[6]

A general defense based on harassing and delaying enemy mobile forces (in order to fatigue, demoralize, and attrit them), while stubbornly defending terrain features and routes that would facilitate decisive counteroffensive operations, made rational military sense.

However, an emotionally charged interpretation of political geography guided Ottoman military deployment. No political figure in Constantinople wanted to confront charges that his fecklessness cost the empire another European province, even if selectively defending territory increased the likelihood of battlefield success. While the Rumelian defense plans Erickson describes predate the political chaos of July 1912, when the Liberal Union coalition replaced the CUP government,[7] neither CUP nor Liberal Union political guidelines permitted sensible adjustment of the helter-skelter deployments. They promoted this political narrative: in eastern Thrace the army must defend Constantinople and hold the historic fortress of Edirne against any Balkan combination, but especially the Bulgars; in the west the army must secure the great, well-provisioned, impenetrable fortress of Yanya to prevent the Greeks from seizing Epirus; Ottoman armies must check the Serbs at the border and positively stop them before Monastir; and foremost, the army must defend Salonika from all enemies while maintaining sufficient troops and artillery in northern Albania to deny Iskodra to the hated Montenegrins. By the way, Kosovo also requires its own independent force.[8] Oh, so many details. Put bluntly, the politicians demanded that the Ottoman army demonstrate an indiscriminant resolve. Upon their word Ottoman Europe would not shrink one more kilometer.

Yet, it shrank to a sliver of Thrace. "Against a single enemy," Erickson concludes, "the strategic problem was solvable, but, against a coalition of enemies attacking each strategic center of gravity simultaneously, the strategic problem was unmanageable."[9]

❖

As Kemal would tell Nuri, facts had to be faced. In late November 1912 survival depended on sustaining operational forces. Shattered units needed time to refit. Reserves arriving from eastern and southern Anatolia needed time to train. An armistice bought time but, to retrieve anything in Europe, Catalca needed to hold and so did Gallipoli.

Ali Fethi was Brigadier General Fahri's chief of staff. Fahri commanded the forces on Gallipoli. On November 25 Kemal became operations officer for the Gallipoli command.[10] Bulgaria had to man its Catalca positions and maintain the siege of Edirne while substantial Bulgarian forces were positioned north of the town of Boyalir, above the narrow neck of the peninsula at the Kava River. Until larger Bulgarian forces arrived, Ottoman troops and fortifications at Boyalir were able to block their advance. However, the Greek navy controlled the Aegean Sea, and that meant amphibious assaults on Gallipoli and the Anatolian shore were an ever-present threat.

Ottoman navy captain Rauf Orbay, who would soon distinguish himself as commander of the cruiser *Hamidiye* in her sallies against Greek shipping, attended a headquarters meeting in Maidos shortly after Kemal became operations officer. The staff was considering various scenarios for defeating an amphibious assault on Gallipoli.

> Some said that if the sandy beaches on the western side were fortified, an invasion force could not be landed, but Mustafa Kemal, who had learnt his lesson from the Italian landings around Benghazi under naval protection, disagreed. He maintained that they had to accept that a landing would be possible under the guns of the enemy fleet, and defense measures would have to be taken after that stage. When the others argued, he grew angry and said "You can put up all the barbed wire you like (on the beach)—I'll smash through it (with naval support). I can easily take the peninsula if there isn't a superior force there to stop me advancing once I've landed."[11]

Erickson, in *Gallipoli: The Ottoman Campaign*, argues convincingly that it was during the First Balkan War "that the Ottomans put together the basic defensive plans and concepts used to defend the peninsula in 1915 against the British." He challenges the dominant historical view that the German advisers led by General Liman von Sanders created the Gallipoli defense plan used in 1915. Fahri's staff, led by Fethi and Kemal, established "four primary defensive groups: one guarding the beaches of the lower peninsula, one guarding the narrow neck of the peninsula [Boyalir], one guarding the Asian beaches [in Anatolia], while one remained in reserve." Fahri stationed the Afyon Reserve Division near Maidos, where Kemal's Nineteenth Division would be positioned in April 1915.[12] This plan reflected the several ideas Kemal advocated during the debate Rauf Orbay witnessed, the key being the division-size reserves positioned near Maidos and prepared to counter a landing force breaking out of a beachhead.

With the December armistice in effect, political infighting between the Liberal Union and the CUP became acute. Mehmed Talat, the CUP power broker, came to Gallipoli to speak to Kemal and Fethi about CUP objectives. They both reacted with suspicion. Falih Rifki Atay, in his memoir of Ataturk, records the caustic Kemal delivering a veiled insult to Talat by asking him "if he would retire from the leadership of the party. 'Why?' replied Talat, Do you want to kill me?' 'No,' replied Mustafa Kemal, 'we'll give you the position you deserve.'" Talat left. Fethi received orders to come to Constantinople. In the capital, CUP leaders revealed to Fethi their plan to overthrow the government and assassinate Nazim Pasha, the Ottoman minister of war. The CUP believed government negotiators would give Edirne to Bulgaria as part of a peace settlement. Fethi refused to participate in murder and the conspirators told him they would not execute the plot. Back in Gallipoli, Fethi told Kemal of the plot and the decision to cancel it. Kemal's response to Fethi was curt: "But they'll do it."[13]

They did. "On 23 January 1913, a great crowd of Unionists advanced on the Porte, shouting slogans calling for the defence of Edirne, and the guards did not stop them because their officers were on the side of the protestors. Two army officers and one police officer who tried to bar their entry were shot. At this point Nazim Pasha came forward shouting 'You have betrayed me!' and was killed by Yekup

Cemil....Enver strode straight up to Kamil Pasha, dictated his resignation, and took the signed document directly to the Sultan."[14] Mahmud Sevket became grand vizier and minister of war, and Cemil became commandant of Istanbul. Sevket was a respected figure; but after the coup Enver, Talat, and Cemil wielded the decisive political power.

Ottoman units in Edirne could not hold out forever, but the fortress's loss had to be weighed against further sacrifice of military forces. The coup leaders, no matter the facts, were committed to military action to relieve Edirne. On February 3, 1913, the First Armistice would expire.

Ottoman and Bulgarian forces never stopped preparing for the next round. In December 1912 the Ottoman general staff proposed a two-pronged attack to retake Edirne. The Gallipoli command, using its provisional force at Boyalir, would attack Bulgarian positions north of the peninsula. The second prong was risky: Provisional Tenth Corps would conduct an amphibious assault at Sarkoy, with the Ottoman navy in the Sea of Marmara providing sealift and fire support. The Provisional Corps would flank enemy forces above Gallipoli. The two prongs would crush the enemy and advance to Edirne. On January 7, 1913, planning began in earnest. Enver, as chief of staff of the Provisional Corps, was deeply involved in the top secret operation. The planners nixed a full-scale troop landing exercise since it would alert the Bulgarians.

On January 12, Ottoman intelligence learned the Bulgarians had reinforced their units along the coast of the Sea of Marmara.[15] At a staff conference on one of the battleships, Kemal voiced severe misgivings about the developing plan. He pointed out that the Bulgarians held the hills above Sarkoy, making a landing dangerous, and that the Boyalir troops could not drive back the Bulgarians who had interior lines and superior numbers. "The scheme sounded all right, but the details had not been properly worked out: they were unworkable. Enver was annoyed. He was the master. He told Mustafa Kemal to talk less and do what he was told."[16]

Kemal considered the terrain, enemy deployment, and enemy operational alternatives. The Bulgarians could easily shift reserves to Boyalir or to Sarkoy; the distance was not great and the road system permitted it. If Ottoman attacks were not synchronized and variables beyond the commander's control could affect synchronization, the Bulgarians would defeat one attack then the other—defeat in detail. Since his staff was planning the Boyalir attack, Kemal's plan likely reflected the latest intelligence.

In January the Bulgarians' newly activated Fourth Army had 92,000 soldiers near Gallipoli and Sarkoy.[17]

Ottoman preparations were stalled by trouble obtaining light craft for the transfer of soldiers and equipment from ships to the beach and, when secured, the Sarkoy piers. On February 1 the Provisional Corps began loading on transport ships. Poor weather and sea conditions created loading difficulties and hampered convoy movement. When the weather cleared on February 3, the troops, after two days aboard the transports, were too weary to conduct an assault. They would set out two days later, the night of February 5.

On February 4 Bulgarian Fourth Army units advanced south toward Boyalir; forces near Sarkoy took the port. By February 6 the Bulgarians had reached the neck of the peninsula, where two Bulgarian regiments entrenched. The delayed amphibious assault had also delayed the Gallipoli attack; the Provisional Force at Boyalir saw its chance to strike first and surprise the Bulgarians vanish.[18]

The decision to attack, however, had powerful advocates; it would not be reversed. Ottoman intelligence estimated the Bulgarians had four batteries of artillery supporting the entrenched regiments. On the morning of February 8, as the Sarkoy assault began, the Provisional Force would attack frontally with two reinforced divisions, each division with two regiments abreast.

The Ottoman divisions attacked with great courage, and though they outnumbered the Bulgarians, the Bulgarians' firepower was unexpectedly fierce. The intelligence estimates were terribly wrong. The

Bulgarians had fourteen artillery batteries supporting the forward regiments, not four; their concentrated fire staggered and then slaughtered the Turkish infantry. "Exaggerating the tactical problem was the terrain itself, which was mostly barren ground with little cover, thus offering the defending Bulgarians excellent fields of fire."[19] Twenty thousand Ottoman soldiers launched the attack and six thousand died.[20] The massacre foreshadowed World War I in which frontal assaults on "entrenched infantry possessing machine guns and modern artillery were doomed to fail, with excessively high casualty rates."[21]

Wind and rough seas off Sarkoy troubled the transport ships the morning of the attack. The men in the landing force heard the battle raging at Boyalir and the fire of massed cannons.

Debarkation began at eleven in the morning of February 8. The initial landing on a sandy, pebbled beach met no opposition; the Bulgarians had retreated into Sarkoy. Ottoman forces headed for Sarkoy to seize the piers so that the Provisional Corps could land artillery and horses, but despite naval gunfire, the Bulgarians thwarted the attack.

"The corps chief of staff, Staff Lieutenant Colonel Enver, departed the beachhead by torpedo boat for Gallipoli at 1 P.M. He would return at 7 P.M., confirming after staff discussions with Staff Major Fethi and Staff Major Mustafa Kemal, the full scope of the [Boyalir] debacle."[22]

On February 9 the Ottomans attacked Sarkoy, driving off the Bulgarians, who shrewdly destroyed the piers as they left. The Provisional Corps had units two kilometers inland by late evening February 9; none of their artillery had landed but the infantry units had fortunately remained within naval gunfire range. Overnight three Bulgarian divisions moved toward Sarkoy and probed the Provisional Corps. General Fahri asked Grand Vizier Sevket to order a withdrawal. Enver objected. Sevket, not threatened by Enver's clout, displayed military wisdom. On February 10 he ordered the Provisional Corps to evacuate. Enver took personal command and did a superior job of successively collapsing the beachhead's covering force, regiments to regiment, regiment to battalions, battalion, company, then the last platoon. Ottoman battleships provided covering fire, but collapsing a bridgehead is a difficult tactical ballet. The cool withdrawal kept the Bulgarians from delivering a destructive attack on the forces ferrying from the beach to the transports. Provisional Corps completed its retreat at 3:30 A.M. on February 11; always aware of media opportunities, even in defeat, Enver was the last man to leave the beach. Ottoman casualties at Sarkoy came to eight killed and thirty-four wounded. At Boyalir, however, the blood had flowed, and flowed in vain.[23]

In the aftermath of the withdrawal, Constantinople created a new Gallipoli General Forces command. Enver pulled rank and made himself its chief operations officer. The new command formed a Boyalir Corps to defend the northern sector against the Bulgarians. Kemal wrote a memo to Sevket, cosigned with Fethi, recommending the Provisional Tenth Corps be assigned to Catalca for use in an offensive to relieve Edirne. The junior staff officers, in other words, went straight to the top with their recommendations. The failed operation had deepened the feud pitting Fethi and Kemal against Enver. Sevket sailed to Gallipoli to personally direct the reorganization; senior officers in the army knew he came to tell his subordinates to end their recriminations and fight the Bulgarians. Their disagreements affected critical operations in what might become the Ottomans' final defense of the capital and the Straits. In the command shuffle, Kemal became chief of staff of the Boyalir Corps.[24]

Ahmet Izzet, acting military commander in chief, decided to send the Tenth Corps to Catalca, convinced by "the wisdom of Mustafa Kemal's memorandum."[25] The professional recriminations were significant, and during the subsequent ten years of Turkish history, they became a grating, personal subtext among the officers involved that lingered to the grave. The *London Times*'s Ataturk obituary of

November 11, 1938, reflected the dispute's significance when it included this remark: "Kemal and Ali Fethi criticized Enver fiercely after the operation at Bulair [Boyalir] failed."

❖

Edirne surrendered March 24. Defending it had sparked the January coup. Its loss now haunted the government, the CUP, and Enver. The First Balkan War would end with Bulgaria gaining Edirne. In return, the treaty gave Ottoman forces control of Thrace to the Enos-Midia Line (Black Sea to the Aegean). Ottoman units from the new Gallipoli Field Army and Catalca advanced to the line. By the end of June 1913 the Ottomans had substantial forces along the new border. The loss of Edirne, however, was too much for the liberals. On June 11, 1913, a group of Liberal Union conspirators murdered Mahmud Sevket in Constantinople as he rode in his chauffeured car. Mehmet Said then became grand vizier. The CUP would eventually execute the murderers.

Hubris and grievance, those classic Balkan devils, would demonstrate that the Edirne question was not settled. Greek control of Salonika and what they regarded as illicit Serbian gains led Bulgaria to attack on its former allies June 29, igniting the Second Balkan War. For Bulgaria it was a disaster. Bulgaria reeled as Serbia and Greece allied with Rumania. Suddenly Bulgaria faced attack on multiple fronts. Rumania seized a chunk of northern Bulgaria and its troops advanced on Bulgaria's capital, Sofia.

With Bulgaria in disarray, on July 22, 1913, the Ottomans moved on Edirne. Enver dashed forward and led the first troops into the city—a personal political victory. Suddenly the sting of the Boyalir-Sarkoy defeat and the First Balkan War loss of Edirne evaporated, at least for its headline hero, Enver.

The Ottoman advance did not end until August 2 when the Gallipoli Field Army's Provisional I Corps, with Kemal as chief of staff, took the port of Dedegac.[26]

Falih Rifki Atay first met Kemal during the Edirne operation in August 1913. Atay came to a corps headquarters at Dimetoka (forty kilometers south of Edirne, now Didymoteicho in Greece). He entered a room and met the commander, Fahri, and Ali Fethi. "On a chair against the opposite wall was a young officer, very blond, handsome, neatly uniformed, keen-eyed, proud, who had been introduced to me as Mustafa Kemal Bey, head of the operations section. He attracted everyone's attention though he did not take much part in the conversation. One could sense that he had an importance disproportionate to his rank.... Kemal was not one of your officers dressed up as daredevil guerrillas, tall cap on head, cartridges all over their chests, hung about with rifles. The esteem in which he was clearly held had to come from merits more solid than these."[27]

What went wrong for the Ottomans? In a series of lectures after the Balkan Wars, Nuri Conker addressed the question and asked Kemal to critique his analysis and add his own thoughts. Kemal's scathing written critique demonstrates why he was held in such high regard—and why he so incited his rivals. Kemal observed that Nuri had called the army's "woeful defeat" in the last war "a painful truth" and "a disappointment." Agreeing with Conker's assessment, he then elaborated, "Yes, it is indeed a painful truth. However there were those, as you too have indicated, who had recognized this ominous truth. And I do believe that one had to have been either derelict or ignorant to have remained unaware of it." He proceeded to enumerate and discuss points from the June 30, 1911, official report to the corps commander in Salonika, in order "to draw a lesson and avoid the continuation of the deep slumber to which we had surrendered ourselves in the past."

Kemal quoted sections of his report about the inadequate training of the forces, the lack of the inspecting commander's knowledge of desired results from basic training, and the passivity of the division commander toward the units, which in turn "incites more detrimental feelings than his complete absence would....He does not know his duty." He continued,

> The ignorance of the regimental and division commanders in their inspections and criticism evokes in the officers feelings of astonishment and, surreptitiously, ridicule and distrust....It is indubitable and indisputable that these regimental and division commanders, with their current mind-set and limited knowledge, would be able to neither train the troops as they should be trained, that is, in accordance with the current military developments, nor give them orders; command or lead them when need arises.
>
> To witness and keep silent about these truths is to endorse the dysfunction of the army, its continued insignificance and its blindness to the vital tasks necessary for the salvation of the nation during war; and that could only be called treason....To try and find a solution to this situation is the duty of any honorable and conscientious person.
>
> What those who lack the authorization to command can do regarding this subject is to submit their observations and investigations to those who have executive authority....
>
> The office to which I submitted this report was occupied by the very same people who had presided over the force that, at the time, had handed over my homeland Salonika to the Greek Army without any resistance.[28]

Kemal's criticism of the surrender of Salonika may be too harsh. The city was lost when the Greeks cracked Ottoman defenses along the Aliakmon River north of Mount Olympus. The Bulgarian army was driving south, and the city and its defending forces faced certain destruction.

The surrender agreement let Ottoman gendarmes and police continue their duties. Many Turkish soldiers were paroled and sent home. Those interned survived the war, and the postwar Ottoman army needed these soldiers.[29]

Nevertheless, Kemal's criticism identified a systemic failure: an army riddled with ill-prepared, unreflective leaders who, instead of building trust between leaders and subordinates, used discord as a management tool. Kemal saw little commitment to military professionalism; patriotism for officers like these was a hollow ritual. Rank for them was higher pay and social prestige, not an increasing level of responsibility. Whether harsh martinets or lazy careerists, they were decadent men. Kemal believed a competent military leader must possess an unwavering moral commitment to duty and demonstrate that commitment through self-discipline, thorough intellectual preparation, and the constant exercise of good judgment.

Kemal described a tactical engagement at Doğan Arslan during the war, in which an officer's ignorance of his duties as a commander, despite his physical courage, produced disaster.

> If, under artillery fire, the regiment had spread out in conformity with the objective and the terrain and had spread out later. And then had launched an attack and had charged within assigned front, had maintained its contact with the neighboring units and had continued to command and control units. And while carrying this out had there been field glasses in hand instead of a saber. And once again had the commander remained close to the regimental reserve, where he could observe and command the situation, rather than being at the front of the skirmish line. Had he reacted the moment he perceived that, although all the necessary precautions and requirements of the situation had been met, and calm and perseverance was firmly in place, through some ill-fated reason his regiment was about to turn back. Had he, disregarding enemy fire, galloped towards the fleeing skirmish line with every intention of running them down. And had he thus halted his regiment and redirected it back towards the enemy. Only then would there have been a great example of courage displayed, befitting a regimental commander, and thus a golden leaf concerning heroism would have been turned in Ottoman history.
>
> The Prophet, himself, would have agreed with the decision to raise a statue in the name of the regimental commander who fell

victim to such courage, and be gladdened by the de facto faith of the [Muslim] community in the concept: "Could the ignorant and the informed ever be the same?"[30]

Kemal criticized the regimental commander for lack of foresight, lack of analysis, and inability to adapt to a changing tactical situation. Lack of intellect, insight, perception, adaptability, and commitment rendered battlefield heroics fruitless. Binoculars in the hands of a professional commander of conscience leading confident soldiers will always defeat a rabble of swords.[31]

CHAPTER 7

The Great War Erupts

YET ANOTHER EUROPEAN WAR LOOMED. ATTACHÉ DUTY IN SOFIA WAS a brief calm before that storm, a false peace as an extended fling. Though Kemal believed his assignment amounted to personal and political exile,[1] he quickly discovered Bulgaria's capital was a very charming, cosmopolitan, and instructive prison. He became a resident of Sofia in November 1913 and for the first time experienced daily life in a Western society. Kemal frequented the city's new cafes and enjoyed its wooded parks. Bulgaria's parliament fascinated him; he studied its political maneuvers as if they were battlefield tactics. The gossips among the ladies attending the weekly dances at the Officers' Club, said he had "the hint of a man of mystery."[2] At night, however, he drank in the bars, and these coarser revels bred a spicier reputation. If the drinking led to debates, "ambition and pride would not let him spare anyone's feelings."[3] Biographer Patrick Kinross argues these were the traits of a man who had not learned self-control and "scorned to conciliate those persons who could make him or mar him"[4]—hardly the traits of a suave diplomat. Yet, Kemal befriended Sava Savoff, the Bulgarian general who defeated the Ottoman forces at Boyalir. The Bulgarians wanted Turkish friends and both countries had scores to settle with Serbia and Greece. Kemal understood that but knew in his head and heart the Bulgarians still coveted Edirne.[5]

After two years of hard war in Africa and Europe, peace was a pleasant interlude, and he enjoyed the reverie. He brushed up on ballroom dance steps and learned to tango. His French improved during his Sofia sojourn: he hired a language tutor to sharpen his skills, and as an attaché, he had time to pursue a regular exchange of letters in French with the widow of a friend in Istanbul, Madame Corinne Lutfu.[6] In Sofia he briefly romanced Dimintrina Kovacheva, the daughter of the Bulgarian minister of war. The Sofia gossips said she rejected his serious advances, but a letter from Kemal to Salih Bozok indicated marriage was not on Kemal's agenda either.[7]

There were unhappy moments. In a letter to Corinne, he wrote, "Winter in Sofia is severe. Our principal recreations are evenings at the Embassy, little parties with colleagues, the occasional game of cards. A routine I do not find agreeable or entertaining." Perhaps his letter to Corinne reflected the dreariness of a cold winter night, yet in the same letter he vowed, "I have ambitions, great ambitions."[8]

Spring in Sofia shone. The pinnacle of Kemal's career as a high-society bon vivant occurred on May 11, 1914, when attended a costume ball at Sofia's swank military club. Fellow partygoers included Bulgaria's King Ferdinand and monocled toffs from the diplomatic community. Kemal wore an old but still stunning Ottoman Janissary soldier's uniform plucked from Constantinople's military museum—remarkably, sent with Ismail Enver's personal permission. Kemal's calculated glare and intense martial presence added dramatic sparks to the fierce warrior's costume. His authentic attire and theatrics created a sensation among the revelers, and—leveraging the social spotlight—he turned the moment into a diplomatic opportunity. Kemal "wrote to his friend Kazim Ozalp, who had arranged the [uniform's] loan...that questions about his dress gave him the opportunity to speak at length of the military prowess and past victories of the Turks."[9]

It was a grand party in the grand style of a Hapsburg-inspired Europe, king and courtiers present, diplomatic and social elites connecting in plush foyers. Kemal with groomed mustache, dressed as a feudal warrior replete with gilded sword and ornate headdress, held his own court. The camera focused; he stood erect and gave a stern yet exotic stare. The antique costume was selected Best of the Ball.

✠

On June 28, 1914, the Hapsburg heir, the Archduke Franz Ferdinand was murdered in Sarajevo by a Serb assassin. The great bloodbath began, and the grand style became history. A month later the declarations began. Austria-Hungary declared war on Serbia July 28. Germany, supporting its ally, declared war on Russia on August 1 and on France on August 3, then invaded Belgium intending to take Paris before Russia could mobilize. Great Britain declared war on Germany, bringing with it the entire Commonwealth, including Canada, Australia, and New Zealand. Montenegro declared war on Austria-Hungary on August 5; France followed suit August 12. Russia declared war on Austria-Hungary August 6. During August the German von Schlieffen Plan cut like a scythe through Belgium as German mobile columns swung south toward the French capital. In the Atlantic, Indian, and Pacific Oceans Britain's Royal Navy hunted German cruisers. British African colonies squared off with Germany's East African possessions.[10] A mad European war gone global confronted Rumania, Bulgaria, Italy, Greece, and the Ottoman Empire.

✠

The Ottomans had sought an alliance as a prop against further disintegration of their European foothold; they had approached France and Russia as well as Britain. Several CUP leaders, especially Enver, favored Germany. Germany, they believed, had no designs on Ottoman territory. Enver offered Germany an alliance on July 22, which Germany rejected. Berlin understood the fractures in Ottoman politics and the impetuous personalities involved. The German foreign ministry thought Turkey "an unsuitable alliance partner"[11] but Kaiser Wilhelm believed a "Balkan grouping" of Rumania, Bulgaria, and Turkey might improve Austria-Hungary's position on the eastern front, as did Austria-Hungary.[12] The kaiser and his Austrian cronies were on to something: when Turkey became a belligerent, "Russia and Britain, in particular, were unprepared for the nearly instantaneous creation of secondary fronts threatening vital strategic interests."[13]

Grand Vizier Said Halim did not foresee a major European war. He thought a war between Austria-Hungary and Serbia would be short and that Bulgaria would join Germany, Austria-Hungary, and Italy in the Triple Alliance with politically and militarily coercing Serbia and Greece the strategic objective.[14] Greece might forfeit parts of western Thrace in any postwar settlement. A limited, defensive alliance with Germany against Russia could keep Turkey out of a general European war, and Russia presented the real, long-standing threat to the Straits. The Ottomans and Germany agreed to such an alliance August 2 and called it the Secret Treaty of Alliance. But as the guns of August blasted Western Europe, Berlin's views shifted: the Ottomans should become a belligerent and go to war. Even a dependent ally was useful, especially one controlling the Straits and denying the Western European allies a sea supply route to Russia.

Kemal disagreed with Constantinople's conventional wisdom. The war would be, by his calculation, a long one. He may have suspected the CUP clique's pro-German sympathies. In the process of assessing Bulgarian reactions to the archduke's assassination and the major powers' mobilization, Ali Fethi and Kemal were inevitably auditing their own government. In an official dispatch to Enver dated July 16, Kemal reported that his "observations in Sofia" indicated the Bulgarians wanted a deal with Austria-Hungary to forward their territorial aims. Constantinople should remain aloof and neutral; if war came the "thing for us to do is provoke a pretext and invade Bulgaria."[15] He may have been trying to steer Enver toward an achievable goal; if Enver needed victory to secure his political position, then he needed to defeat Bulgaria in a border war. Enver's ambitions, however, extended beyond Bulgaria. With good reason his friends nicknamed him "Napoleonlik."[16] In September, a very blunt Kemal wrote Salih Bozok that "we have declared mobilization without fixing our objective. This is very dangerous.... Looking at Germany's position from a military point of view, I am by no means certain she will win this war. True, the Germans have overrun strong fortifications at lightning speed and are advancing towards Paris. But the Russians are pushing to the Carpathians and are pressing hard the Germans' Austrian allies. The Germans will thus have to set aside a part of their forces to aid the Austrians. Seeing this, the French will counter-attack and put pressure on the Germans. The Germans will then have to recall their troops from the Austrian front. It is because an army which zig-zags to and fro must come to a sad end that I do not feel certain about the outcome of this war."[17]

Berlin and Enver needed a binding incident to solidify an open German-Ottoman alliance—especially one with riveting imagery— and the flight of *Goeben* provided it. On August 4 the German battle cruiser *Goeben* and light cruiser *Breslau*, after shelling Bone and Phillipeville in French Algeria on August 3, evaded French and British naval forces and sneaked into Messina, Italy, to take on coal. At Messina, Rear Admiral Wilhelm Souchon, the kaiser's Mediterranean squadron commander, received instructions to make for the Dardanelles. His ships left Messina, shook British pursuers, then bolted through the Aegean. On August 10, after conferring with a German officer who demanded he let the ships enter the Straits, Enver gave Souchon permission. He did not consult the cabinet.[18] The *Goeben*'s sortie was conspiracy at its most dramatic. As *Goeben* passed the Ottoman forts lining the Narrows, the fast, heavily armed warship instantly became the most powerful naval vessel in the Sea of Marmara.

Suspecting Ottoman intentions, on August 1, Great Britain's first lord of the Admiralty, Winston Churchill, had halted delivery of two new warships to the Ottoman navy.[19] The Ottoman government fanned national outrage by accusing the British of breaking the warship contract and insulting the Ottoman people. The two German ships that had arrived would replace the vessels "stolen" by the perfidious British. In a false nod to British and French demands to uphold the laws of neutrality, Constantinople announced it had purchased the German warships and renamed them *Yavuz Sultan Selim* and *Midilli*. Ottoman flags replaced the German pennants; the German sailors, however, simply remained on board, donning red-felt fezzes with black tassels in lieu of their peakless blue sea caps. This transparent ruse angered the British government and drew cynical but approving smirks from the Germans. Russian, French, and British observers concluded that the fact German crews remained on board the warships demonstrated that the "Germans were running the Turkish army and navy. As some wit in the Constantinople diplomatic corps said, it was 'Deutschland uber Allah.'"[20]

The Ottomans told the Germans they could not fully mobilize their military until spring 1915. September came and Germany failed to win decisive victories on its eastern and western fronts. Germany needed to distract the British and Russians. In October the Germans insisted the Ottomans act and asked them to attack Russian seaports with the Ottoman navy to open a Caucasus front, and from Sinai, to threaten the Suez Canal. Enver agreed. Mehmed Talat and Ahmet Cemal accepted his decision.[21] On October 29 and 30, the German-manned *Yavuz* (*Goeben*) led a strike force that shelled Sevastopol and Odessa. Details regarding the naval attacks remain uncertain, but the action provoked Russia, which declared war on November 2, 1914. Britain and France followed suit November 5. The British declaration was perfunctory; on November 3 a Royal Navy squadron opened fire on two outer forts protecting the Dardanelles, Kumkale (on the western tip of the Dardanelles' Anatolian shore) and Seddulbahir. A heavy shell penetrated Seddulbahir's magazine and the explosion smashed the castle, knocking its ten coastal guns off their mountings.[22] On November 11 Constantinople formally declared war on the Triple Alliance. The Ottomans became a Central Power, the decayed yet imperial Osmans aligning themselves with Austria-Hungary's Habsburgs and Germany's Hohenzollerns. "With hindsight," historian Hew Strachan writes, "Turkey's entrance into the war was ordained from the moment it admitted the *Goeben* and *Breslau* to the Dardanelles."[23]

✦

Kemal desperately sought a command. In his September letter to Salih Bozok he said he had approached Enver directly. "If for any reason they do not want to allow me to return let them say so clearly and I will then decide my course of action."[24] He had tempered his correspondence to Enver, as rhetorically supplicant and beseeching as his pride would permit. Enver ignored him with an aristo-bureaucratic pirouette: the Bulgarian post is vital, you're our man in Sofia, warm regards. Kemal now considered resigning his commission and enlisting; if denied binoculars, he would demand a rifle. The Sofia interlude was over.

✦

In November 1914, Russia attacked in the Caucasus, but the Ottoman army halted the offensive. Enver, envisioning glory, left Constantinople for the eastern front. As minister of war he would assume command of the Ottoman's first offensive. On December 25 his Third Army attacked Sarkamis. The temperatures dropped to -30 degrees C. The Russians counterattacked and the Ottomans lost 30,000 dead; 7,000 were captured. Enver's foray ended in abject failure. "Enver's ambitions, both for himself and Turkey," Hew Strachan dryly observes, "were Napoleonic; his abilities—at least as a commander—were not."[25]

With Enver in the Caucasus, his deputy, Ismail Hakki, answered Kemal's latest request. Hakki's telegram ordered Kemal "to leave immediately to assume command of the Nineteenth Division."[26] The orders told him to come to Constantinople and Kemal left Sofia January 20, 1915. At the War Ministry in Constantinople he inquired: Where is the Nineteenth Division? He received a dull reply: "There might be such a division in Liman von Sanders army, go and see him."[27]

Kemal's search for the division took him to Liman von Sanders's chief of staff, Kazim. "There's no such division," Kazim said. "But it may be there are plans for it in the Third Army Corps we are creating in Gallipoli. Perhaps if you go there. But first let me introduce you to the general."[28]

Kazim ushered Kemal into Liman von Sanders's office. The general greeted him courteously despite Kemal's prickly reputation for anti-German opinions. Then the general, aware Kemal had just left Sofia, made the mistake of asking Kemal his assessment of Bulgarian intentions:

"Aren't the Bulgarians coming in yet?"
"As far as I can see they won't be coming in for awhile."
"Why not?"
"As I see it, they won't enter the war until they see convincing evidence that Germany can win, or until the fighting actually touches their territory."
Von Sanders bristled. Then, thinking rather than reacting, smiled and said: "Have the Bulgars no confidence in Germany's victory?"
"No, your Excellency," Kemal answered.
Von Sanders' face reddened. "Why? How can this be?"
"That's how it is, sir."
"And what is your opinion."[29]

Kemal would later tell Atay that he could not demur, despite the awkward situation: "I examined my conscience for a moment and answered, 'I think the Bulgars are right.' [Liman von Sanders] at once stood up and dismissed me."[30]

Kemal left to contact his division's cadre and begin turning a paper formation the War Ministry could not find into a combat unit with discipline and grit.

Ataturk with his sister Makbule Atadan and mother Zubeyde Hanim. Taken one day after graduation from the Staff College. Ataturk wears his general staff captain's uniform. (The Turkish Ministry of Culture and Tourism)

A dapper Ataturk with fellow Ottoman army officers in Beirut. The fezzes, mustaches, dress uniforms, cavalry sabers, palm, and ornate chairs make this photo a classic. It was probably taken in July 1906. Ali Fuad (Cebesoy) is standing at the left rear.

A photo taken of the French Army's Picardy Maneuvers, fall 1910. French colonel Auguste Edouard Hirschauer lectures. Ataturk is immediately behind him. Note the collection of foreign officers. The French employed aircraft in the large-scale war game and everyone was interested. Ali Fethi Okyar is to Ataturk's left.

A Turco-Italian War photo of Ataturk with Arab tribesman at Derna, Cyrenaica (modern eastern Libya). The photo was taken in 1912. Note that the tribesmen are armed with a variety of rifles—all of them likely scavenged from the battlefield. (The Ataturk Mausoleum [Anitkabir])

Ataturk in the uniform of an Ottoman janissary soldier. The janissary uniform is authentic. Ataturk wore the uniform to a costume ball in Sofia, Bulgaria in 1914. (The Ataturk Mausoleum [Anitkabir])

Ataturk in a trench at Gallipoli, sometime in August 1915. The trench position may have been on Chunuk Bair. Ataturk, with his binoculars ready for immediate use, gives the cameraman a poised and dramatic profile. The Turkish soldier's fierce glare (at the right) seems a bit more candid. (The Ataturk Mausoleum [Anitkabir])

Ataturk at Gallipoli. This photo was taken while he was serving as commander of the Anafartalar Group. (Turkish military website, Galllipoli archive)

Ataturk with his corps commander at Gallipoli, Essat Pasha. Essat Pasha stands to the right of Ataturk. The German officer behind them is Colonel Hans Kannengiesser. (Turkish military website, Galllipoli archive)

A photo of Ataturk in full military dress taken near the end of World War I. His hat is a kalpak. (The Ataturk Mausoleum [Anitkabir])

Ataturk meets with Rauf Orbay at the Sivas Congress, September 1919. Rauf became an Ottoman naval hero in the First Balkan War.

Ataturk and Ismet Inonu inspect a platoon from one of the assault battalions (tücum Tabun) at Eskisehir. The photo is dated June 22, 1921. (The Ataturk Mausoleum [Anitkabir])

Ataturk and part of his command group observe the Great Offensive from Koca Tepe. This photo was taken August 26, 1922, as the offensive against Greek forces in Anatolia began. The optical device is a binocular periscope, sometimes called "trench binoculars."

Ataturk with his aides-de-camp. The photo was taken in the summer of 1922. Ataturk's friend Salih Bozok stands behind Ataturk's right shoulder. (The Ataturk Mausoleum [Anitkabir])

Ataturk walks with Kazim Karabekir (to Ataturk's right, looking down) and Fevzi Cakmak (thumb tucked in coat). The photo dates from January 1923. The three men were senior leaders in the Turkish War of Independence. After World War I, Karabekir commanded Turkish military forces in eastern Anatolia. These forces served as the backbone of Kemal's nationalist movement.

Latife Hanim (Ataturk's wife), Ismet Inonu, and Ataturk. The photo was taken in Ankara in 1923.

The general becomes the statesman. Ataturk addresses a crowd of Turkish citizens in Bursa in September 1924. (The Turkish Ministry of Culture and Tourism)

CHAPTER 8

Gallipoli

JANUARY, FEBRUARY, AND MARCH 1915 WERE BUSY MONTHS IN LONDON as well as on the Gallipoli Peninsula. British admirals, generals, their advisers, and First Lord of the Admiralty Winston Churchill examined the depth charts, scrutinized fortifications, and analyzed the naval minefields. After rancorous debate, by January 8, 1915, they had persuaded themselves that the French and British navies had the armor, speed, and firepower to smash through the Dardanelles. The Allied battleships would then train their guns on Constantinople, which might capitulate rather than suffer certain destruction from shell fire delivered by the 1915 version of intercontinental ballistic missiles. Clearing the Bosporus would open the route to Russia; and dropping hints of territorial adjustments at the Ottomans' expense might lead Bulgaria and Greece to join the Allied cause. If Germany would not sue for peace, it would have to send significant ground forces east to face these new Balkan allies, thus ending the lethal stalemate on the western front.

Mass slaughter was the real concern. Industrial-age reinforced concrete, barbed wire, munitions, and heavy weapons—and millions of quickly mobilized soldiers jammed into northern France and Belgium—produced static warfare and hideous, unimaginable human casualties. An unbroken and apparently unbreakable trench-and-bunker system zigzagged from the Swiss border to the English Channel. Operational mobility had vanished. The war in the west had become an endless series of frontal assaults, the doomed formations crossing the cratered strip between the armies, the no-man's-land, were decimated by massed artillery and machine guns supported by dug-in rifle regiments. Five hundred belt-fed rounds per minute from the barrel of a Maxim gun butchered esprit de corps and vanquished the will to win. The unrelenting horror drove Churchill and his advisers to gamble on the great naval assault.

In early February Kemal arrived in Tekirdag on the Sea of Marmara between Constantinople and Boyalir, where the Nineteenth Division was forming. He discovered his division had one regiment, the Fifty-seventh, instead of its authorized three; its other two regiments, the Fifty-eighth and Fifty-ninth, had been assigned to Ottoman Sixth Corps.[1] According to his report of January 1917, "The Allied threat to the Dardanelles allowed no time to bring the division up to strength, and I was ordered on February 25 to proceed to Maidos at the head of the 57th Regiment."[2]

Maidos lies on the Dardanelles as the strait enters Marmara, northeast of the Narrows. The Allied navies attacked the Aegean entrance to the strait on February 19, 1915, and encountered improved defenses. The Ottomans had learned from the November 1914 Seddulbahir disaster: they remounted Seddulbahir's guns and hardened other forts. The defenders positioned mobile howitzer batteries on both sides of the strait to reinforce the forts and to subject warships, especially Allied minesweepers, to plunging fire. The Ottomans ultimately deployed over 400 of them in eleven serial belts stringing the strait. Barreling through the strait without clearing the mines was madness; large naval mines fractured the hulls of the era's most heavily armored warships. British naval theorist Sir Julian Corbett, using the figure of 350 mines, estimated that—if unswept—"only one of sixteen allied battleships could reasonably hope to reach the Sea of Marmara."[3] Minesweeping the Dardanelles was tedious business, troubled by the five-knot head current drifting toward the Aegean, and made all but impossible when trawlers faced unsuppressed, direct-fire coastal guns and high-angle fire from howitzers concealed in the hills.

The February 19 bombardment, led by the superdreadnought *Queen Elizabeth,* lasted eight hours and achieved little. Briefly foiled by bad weather, the ships returned February 25 to attack the outer forts with inconclusive results.[4] To supplement the bombardment, on March 4 Royal Marines raided Seddulbahir and Anatolia's Kumkale forts and destroyed several guns. Steady naval attacks continued. Frustrated admirals sent the *Queen Elizabeth* north to Gaba Tepe, a headland jutting from the peninsula's Aegean coast midway between the strait's entrance and Boyalir. She fired her eight 15-inch rifles over Gallipoli's ridges and bombarded the Kilitbahir and Canakkale fortifications.[5] The long-range heavy gun barrage—attractive in theory—drilled holes in the water and dug a few impressive craters; the forts defending the inner Narrows remained intact. The ongoing battle began to turn in the defenders' favor as the Ottoman Dardanelles artillery batteries sank or damaged several minesweepers. The night of March 13 mobile howitzers, using observers aided by searchlights, wreaked hell on the minesweeping squadron, damaging four minesweepers and an escorting cruiser.[6] March 18 proved conclusive. A French battleship hit a mine and sank. That day the Allies lost two other battleships and three more were badly damaged. The navy-only strategy had failed.[7]

As the Allied naval attacks progressed, Kemal's Nineteenth Division received two additional regiments, the Seventy-second and Seventy-seventh, both manned by Arab conscripts. Kemal put the division through a series of tough training exercises. The Fifth Army had good reason to expect further assaults. "The abortive naval phase of the Anglo-French attack was obviously finished.... But daily intelligence reports hammered home the hard truth that the humiliated British and French intended to recoup, and soon."[8]

The French and British knew the minefields were their nemesis. Infantry landings to capture the Narrows' forts would allow the slow, ungainly minesweepers to clear the channel. An amphibious attack was a larger, more complex gamble, but one more likely to succeed.

The defenders watched the Allies' preparations. "From early April, British and French ships loaded with troops and supplies converged on the Greek island of Lemnos, eighty kilometres from the [Dardanelles'] entrance. The invasion plan was perhaps the worst-kept secret of the entire war."[9] Kemal would tell Rusen Esref Unaydin in his series of interviews, "Conversations with Anafartalar Commander Mustafa Kemal," that he was certain "if the enemy were to attempt a disembarkation he would attempt it at two points [on the Gallipoli Peninsula], one at Seddulbahir and the other at Gaba Tepe."[10] Kemal indicated he had identified the two likely landing sites in 1914 after reflecting on his Balkan War Gallipoli experience. From its position at Maidos, the Nineteenth could reinforce both the central (Gaba Tepe) and southern (Cape Helles) sectors.

❖

The moon set at 2:57 A.M. on the morning of April 25, 1915. A heavy darkness descended on Gallipoli, remaining until 4:05 A.M. when dawn's first gray edge filtered over the eastern ridge lines. At 4:29 A.M. an Ottoman sentry rose from a trench on Ariburnu Point, north of Gaba Tepe, and saw thirty-six large rowboats approaching the narrow beach. The sentry and his detachment, "after some seconds of disbelief," fired their rifles at the boats as their keels scraped the shallows.[11] The Australian and New Zealand Army Corps (ANZAC) invaders had intended to land at Gaba Tepe, but with the tricky sea approach and pitch darkness they missed that more southerly shoreline. Lucky for them—at Gaba Tepe the Turks had dug in. The Australian and New Zealand soldiers quickly drove the Ottoman defenders off Ariburnu's beach and up into the rugged hills. On the far side of those imposing hills lay the exposed rear of the forts protecting the Narrows and covering the lines of naval mines. The Narrows forts were the core of the Ottoman defense.[12] Whether a surprised defender or a temporarily disoriented invader, as the infantry clashed, the battle had begun in deadly earnest.

Otto Liman von Sanders, the German diplomat and military adviser to the Ottomans who commanded the Ottoman Fifth Army at Gallipoli, assessed the April 25 attack in his memoir, *Five Years in Turkey:* "The preparations of the enemy were excellent, their only defect being they were based on reconnaissances that were too old and they underestimated the powers of resistance of the Turkish soldier." The Allied preparations included the appearance of twenty large ships in the Aegean Sea's Gulf of Saros off Boyalir. The threat to the peninsula's narrow throat was explicit. Small boats left the transports, then withdrew. The maneuver briefly fooled Liman von Sanders, or gave him pause until he determined the action was a feint. Hesitation was the demonstration's operational intent: to sow confusion and delay the deployment of Ottoman reinforcements to the genuine invasion sites. As the hours passed, Fifth Army headquarters learned that enemy forces had landed down the peninsula, from Ariburnu to Cape Helles. Liman von Sanders remembered that Third Corps' commander Essad Pasha (Kemal's corps commander) arrived at his headquarters with detailed reports, including the disturbing revelation that the enemy had seized the Sari Bair heights above Ariburnu. Essad assured him that the Nineteenth Division "was on the march," heading for the critical ground. By day's end, he had received a stack of reports indicating the massive Allied operation involved nearly two hundred ships, a floating colossus of supplies and firepower behind the enemy amphibious beachheads. The Fifth Army had to hold the ridges above them. News of a particular mountain battlefield success encouraged him—the Nineteenth Division had "driven back the enemy troops" in the Ariburnu sector.[13]

❖

The Nineteenth Division paid for its mountain in blood.

Three years later Kemal, drinking coffee and chain-smoking fragrant, thick cigarettes, told Unaydin how on horseback he had led his troops from their assembly area at Bigali up to Koja Chemen Tepe (Hill 971):

> Imagine it, the highest point on the peninsula...the Arıburnu shore was in a blind spot and could not be observed, but I could see many boats and warships on the water. The enemy infantry has landed. It is difficult to move, because of the [steep and gullied] terrain....My men grew tired, walking uphill. I spoke to the regimental and battery commander and told them to give the men a little rest. Take ten minutes then follow me. I walked towards Chunuk Bair with the regimental doctor, the commander of the mountain artillery battery, and my lieutenant....We left the animals and reached Chunuk Bair on foot....The scene before me...I think this is the most important moment.

At that point Kemal lit another cigarette and reflected, before addressing that most important moment.

In the military engagement on Chunuk Bair and Battleship Hill, the ridge just below it, Kemal halted the fleeing Ninth Division soldiers with a crisp order to attach bayonets and lie down. At Boyalir the Allies had feinted with its battleships; here Kemal feinted with bayonets to confuse an enemy company and purchase five minutes. The tactical feint stalled the Australians, buying time for the arrival of his Fifty-seventh Regiment, which eventually received Kemal's most famous command: "I do not expect you to attack, I order you to die! In the time which passes until we die, other troops and commanders can take our place!"[14]

Kemal would say much later, in that uncomfortable way he had of presenting harsh, plain fact: "The Fifty-seventh Regiment is a famous regiment...because they all died."[15]

※

At 9:40 A.M. Kemal sent the First and Second Battalions of the Fifty-seventh into combat below Chunuk Bair, keeping the Third as a reserve. The Twenty-seventh Regiment of the Ninth Division, in contact with the ANZACs, received orders from its commander, Colonel Halil Sami, to coordinate with Kemal.[16]

The battle for the slopes continued, hectic and chaotic. The fighting from Battleship Hill (or Baby 700, the hill just below it) to Chunuk Bair (Hill 850) for the ANZACs was a lethal staircase.[17] British major general and respected counterinsurgency expert C. E. Callwell, writing five years after the battle, captured the confusion both sides experienced, but particularly that of the ANZACs:

> It is difficult to give a connected account of the disjointed encounters that took place during this day of fluctuating battle. The further the assailants pushed inland from the beach the more difficult the terrain became, and the more formidable the resistance of the antagonists, who displayed marked skill in utilizing the plentiful cover afforded by the scrub and by the very broken character of the ground. There had been intermingling of [ANZAC] companies and battalions even at the moment of the first rush from the beach, and this naturally became aggravated during a succession of haphazard, but sanguinary, affrays in gullies and on the hillsides. In the eagerness of pursuit, parties of Australians pushed far ahead, became isolated, and were swallowed up in the ravines by the much stronger bodies of Osmanlis.[18]

Around 1 P.M. the Twenty-seventh and the Fifty-seventh Regiments launched a vigorous attack on the Australians. Kemal brought up the Seventy-second and Seventy-seventh Regiments (newly assigned to the Nineteenth Division), the former to reinforce the Twenty-seventh and the latter for his own right flank. The four Ottoman regiments were then arrayed in a 180-degree arc, pressing the eight Australian ones, whose advances were halted by the Turkish assault. Kemal kept his corps commander, Essad Pasha, and the Twenty-seventh Regiment commander informed by courier.[19]

Essad was a capable soldier and a flexible senior leader who trusted his on-the-spot division commanders. As the situation clarified, Essad from his headquarters at Mal Tepe made an excellent operational decision, one assuring unity of command in his corps' two main battle sectors: he put Kemal in charge of the entire threatened sector, naming him Ariburnu Front Commander, and attached the Twenty-seventh Regiment to his Nineteenth Division. Based on the dire situation at Chunuk Bair, Kemal had already taken effective control of the Twenty-seventh. Essad had the martial insight to ratify that officially and then designate command responsibility for the diverging battle sectors. Sami and the rest of his Ninth Division would concentrate on enemy forces to the south at Cape Helles. Kemal would focus on Ariburnu.[20]

The fluid combat at Ariburnu exposed Kemal to both observation and fire—binoculars don't ward off bullets. C. E. W. Bean records an incident reported by Australian soldiers below Battleship Hill (Baby 700): "The higher hill, of which the lower slopes faced them across the valley, was the shoulder of Chunuk Bair, a commanding height which, even more truly than Hill 971, was the key of the main ridge. On its skyline, which the men could see about 900 yards away on their left front as they lay in the scrub, was a solitary tree. By the tree stood a man, to and from whom went several messengers." An Australian officer "fired at him, but the flick of the bullets could not be seen in the scrub, and the officer did not move."[21]

Chaos and fear do not breed certainty, and Bean, who saw action at Gallipoli as a combat reporter for the *Sydney Morning Herald*, understood that positive identification of the officer as Kemal was not possible. Likely? Yes. Kemal used the position as a command center and was constantly dispatching messengers.

Ferocious attacks continued through the dust and gravel gullies, up and down the naked heights, gains reversed in minutes as enemy artillery pounded a penetration and the momentarily victorious attackers scattered, pulled back to a rock, a hole, a hasty trench, anything to shield them from the withering shrapnel. Then they might take a sip of water from a canteen, regroup, and—when the sergeant passed the word—attack again. An Australian unit, after launching its second all-out assault on Baby 700, reported seeing Turkish soldiers retreating, "one of them lumbering back over the shoulder of the hill with a machine-gun packed upon a mule."[22] The Turk and his machine gun—and a thousand men like him—would retreat, reorganize, receive orders from Kemal, and, in turn, deliver another counterattack.

As night fell the ANZACs outnumbered the Turks at Ariburnu by at least two to one. The Turks, however, were receiving reinforcements. In the early hours of April 26, aboard a battleship offshore, Commonwealth commanders considered evacuating the beachhead. They decided to stick it out. General Sir Ian Hamilton, the overall Allied commander, advised the troops to "dig dig dig."[23]

Kemal received a mountain artillery battalion on April 26, when the Sixty-fourth and Thirty-third Regiments arrived from Asia. He spent that day resting his troops while shelling the ANZACs. The fresh troops were in Kemal's line on April 27. That night, the Sixty-fourth and what was left of the Fifty-seventh Regiment attacked the ANZAC perimeter from the north. Once the Aussies reacted, the other four regiments struck from the south. Kemal kept no reserve. "The Turks broke into the enemy trenches but the attacking regiments, exhausted and depleted from two days of combat, could not break through." The Ottoman Fifth Division arrived. Despite artillery ammunition shortages, on May 1, 1915, Kemal's forces, now some

18,000 men, attacked again. Fighting was hand to hand yet the Allies held. Kemal considered calling off the offensive when "in the early afternoon an Ottoman radio detachment intercepted an Australian transmission that indicated their tactical situation was critical." Both sides were exhausted, but neither was beaten. That night the Turks attacked again, meeting fierce resistance. At 3 A.M. on May 2 Kemal "acknowledged failure and called off the attacks." The Ottomans had lost 6,000 soldiers.[24]

Liman von Sanders began reorganizing his forces. Kemal was commanding a corps-sized formation with a divisional headquarters. The ad hoc arrangement made sense in an emergency but was unwieldy, so Essad assumed direct control of the Ariburnu front on May 5. Enver wrote Liman von Sanders, declaring that the Gallipoli battles were of utmost importance to the state. Massive reinforcements arrived. Essad Pasha, his new Northern Force now fielding 50,000 soldiers, planned a major attack for 3:30 A.M. May 19. He intended to crush the ANZAC defense with one vast wave of soldiers descending from the dark cliffs to the Ariburnu beachhead. Surprise was essential. Kemal's division would strike from the north. Kemal put the Sixty-fourth Regiment on his right flank, the Fifty-seventh on his left, and asked both to select thirty men to maintain contact among themselves and the Fifth Division on their southern flank.

But if it can go wrong, it will. Royal Naval Air Service aircraft spotted Ottoman reinforcements in transit. On May 18 the ANZACs noticed a lull in Turkish artillery fire, and to veteran soldiers this was a signal the enemy was conserving ammunition for an attack. Allied commanders ordered the ANZACs to stand-to in their trenches; at 3 A.M. on May 19 the Ottomans had darkness but not surprise.

The Fifty-seventh Regiment seized parts of the first Australian trench, but the ANZACs foiled the 30,000 man assault. The battle became a to-and-fro slaughter, with the Australians counterattacking.

Royal Navy gunfire disrupted Ottoman reserves. The Fifty-seventh held but at 3:30 P.M. Kemal ordered its withdrawal. The vast wave had failed. The Fifth Army reported Essad's force lost 3,368 and 5,967 were wounded—one in three of the assault force had become a casualty.[25]

The stench of decaying bodies haunted the battlefield. On May 24 the Ottomans and ANZACs agreed to a temporary truce. It was a dismal, necessary duty. During the truce, Kemal allegedly posed as a member of a burial detail in order to get a close, personal look at Australian positions.[26] He probably did. Australian soldiers complained that German officers commanding Ottoman forces spied on their trenches during the armistice, yet they admitted they too "had a look at theirs."[27]

Kemal received a German Iron Cross on May 23—he might dislike Germans, but Germans recognized his courage. On June 1 he was promoted to full colonel.

◈

After the May 19 debacle, the Ariburnu front "entered a period of relative quiet," but Kemal was not a quiet commander.[28] He led an attack on May 29. The ANZACS struck back June 5. Talat then Enver traipsed through Gallipoli—it was their nation's western front. Kemal launched another assault June 29 and 30. The Ottomans suffered one thousand casualties in the operation.

Enver rebuked Kemal for the action and "cancelled his appointment as acting corps commander."[29] Serious fighting continued at Cape Helles, but the Anglo-French strategic gamble had failed. Instead of breaking the western front deadlock, the strategy had brought the stalemate east. Now time ticked by for the soldiers at Ariburnu as it did for the unfortunates at Ypres, time measured in night patrols with knives, pistols, and grenades, around-the-clock sniping, and field artillery concentrations. The immediate presence and participation of warships was a distinction in terms of concentrated big-gun firepower, though on the western front heavy naval cannons were cropping up on armored trains.

❖

The big bang of August 6, 1915, completely destroyed the relative quiet as Commonwealth forces launched a long anticipated offensive. The Fifth Army knew an offensive lurked, having noticed in July a steady troop and supply buildup. Throughout the day the Allies launched savage attacks at Cape Helles and Ariburnu. At 10 P.M. on August 6 they added a surprise: an amphibious assault immediately north of Ariburnu at Suvla Bay. The landing extended the beachhead and gave Allied forces new avenues to attack the Sari Bair ridge. Kemal immediately understood the fatal threat the Suvla Bay thrust presented to the Ottomans' northern (right flank) defense, but he had trouble enough in his division's Battleship Hill sector.[30] On August 6 the First Australian Division attacked the southern edge of Sari Bair from positions north of Gaba Tepe, igniting the Battle of Lone Pine (what the Turks called the Battle of Kanli Sirt). The main effort began August 7 at 1:30 A.M. with Chunuk Bair and Hill 971 its objectives. The battles in Chunuk Bair's broken terrain quickly became chaotic. Several ad hoc Ottoman battle groups fenced with the ANZACs. On August 8 an ANZAC attack smashed through trenches held by the weary Ottoman Fourteenth Regiment positioned on Chunuk Bair. The New Zealand brigade took Chunuk Bair and held it despite suffering grievous losses as fire from Ottoman units on Hill 971 raked their lines.

Liman von Sanders ordered two divisions from Boyalir under the command of Colonel Ahmet Feyzi to reinforce the Suvla Bay–Ariburnu front and counterattack. The divisions marched over thirty kilometers. On August 8 Feyzi himself reached Chunuk Bair and reported a counterattack by the Sixty-fourth Regiment had thrown the ANZACs off the crest. Feyzi's divisions arrived fatigued. He requested time to rest, which infuriated Liman von

Sanders who phoned Kemal that night. The German general had decided to give

> command of all the troops in the Anafartalar section to Colonel Mustapha Kemal Bei, commander of the 19th Division, which was the farthest north on the Ariburnu front. Mustapha Kemal…was a leader that delighted in responsibility. On the morning of April 25th he had attacked with the 19th Division on his own initiative, drove the advancing enemy back to the coast and then remained for three months in the Ariburnu front tenaciously and inflexibly resisting all attacks. I had full confidence in his energy.[31]

Liman von Sanders remembered that Kemal's command

> defended ground from the northern slopes of the Kiretch Tepe [northeast of Suvla Bay] to Koja Chemen Tepe, inclusive.…It consisted of six divisions. In this front which crossed the Anafartalar plain and was parallel to the coast, all commanding heights were in the hands of the Turks and crowned by Turkish artillery. Unfortunately, the artillery was neither numerous nor modern, barring the field guns, and ammunition was short. Otherwise the British would not have been able to remain long in the lower portions of this front.[32]

Edward Erickson argues pragmatism drove the decision as well: "Kemal was intimately familiar with the ground and the units involved in the fight for Sari Bair. He had been in action on the ANZAC perimeter since April 25 and since early May had commanded the northern shoulder of Essad's Northern Group. As such, the Sari Bair ridge fell in Kemal's 'tactical backyard.'"

Erickson also points to the notorious Sazlidere discussion—a debate marked by the usual one-two punch of Kemal's astute vision and courage of conviction. The Sazlidere ravine lay on the northern end of the perimeter. "The *dere* was more like a narrow gully, choked in thick scrub."[33] Kemal said the ravine gave enemy units a masked and poorly defended approach to Hill 971. Worse—from a leadership perspective—the gully lay on a command boundary line; attackers always seek command boundaries for they are gray zones of responsibility. Kemal sent a polite (by his standards) note to Essad on July 18 asking for a boundary clarification between his command and the Anafartalar area (which was commanded by a German, Major Wilhelm Willmer). Essad rejected Kemal's assessment and replied, "Little valleys like this cannot be inclusive or exclusive of either side (i.e., either command)." Kemal fired back a letter: "The enemy could try a night assault by an assault group directed up Sazlidere" toward the Sari Bair ridge, and a unit connecting the Ariburnu front to the Anafartalar sector would "get no help from the Nineteenth Division's reserve in the valleys to the south of Duztepe (Battleship Hill)." Kemal speculated that small, bold reconnaissance parties would advance through the gully to the high ground.[34] Essad agreed to come see Kemal and hear his analysis. According to Kemal, Essad listened, then "patted my shoulder. 'Don't you worry, he [the enemy] can't do it,' he said. Seeing that it was impossible for me to put over my point of view I felt it unnecessary to prolong the argument any further."[35]

But prior to the ANZAC assault the New Zealand Auckland Mounted Rifles had indeed probed the Sazlidere cut and the British Commonwealth commanders learned the northern sector was vulnerable.[36] Liman von Sanders likely knew of the letters and (now that the enemy had launched a successful northern attack) Kemal's prescience.

Kemal now had a major command in the most critical sector and he attacked. Liman von Sanders remembered August 9, as Kemal "took command of the thrice ordered attack on both sides of the Azmak Dere and pushed the enemy back toward the coast in several places."[37] Commonwealth forces, however, retained key terrain and reinforcements continued to arrive. The day when Feyzi failed to attack could not be retrieved, now Liman von Sanders knew the Anafartalar sector faced another crisis.[38]

At 4 A.M. on August 9 one of Kemal's new divisions, the Twelfth, advanced 2,000 meters and ran into the advancing British Thirty-second Brigade near Tekke Tepe, east of Suvla Bay. The British retreated in disorder. Attacks continued throughout the day. The British attacked Chunuk Bair in the late afternoon, driving through the Ottoman Twenty-fourth Regiment. Kemal had ordered this regiment, commanded by his friend Nuri Conker, to defend Chunuk Bair. "Nuri could not prevent the temporary loss of Conk Bayiri, but his role in the fighting was remembered later when Ataturk chose for him the surname Conker (Man of Conk)."[39] By the day's end Liman von Sanders concluded that Kemal had stabilized the Anafartalar front, and he notified Enver.[40] Kemal, going without sleep, planned another attack for 4:30 A.M. August 10. The Eighth Division would conduct the main assault with three others in support. A wave of men would sweep across the Sari Bair ridge, with a specific concentration on the crest and flanks of Chunuk Bair, and Kemal would personally lead the attack, not with his sword but with his riding crop.

Kemal sneaked forward with his reconnaissance teams. Ottoman artillery preparatory fires began and abruptly ended. Lying prone on the rock and dirt he waited and—as planned—machine guns and direct fire artillery slammed the Commonwealth lines before him. "At the exact moment when the firing ceased he raised himself up and pointed to the enemy line with his riding crop." All told, sixteen Ottoman battalions hit the allied lines. "It was a massive blow and the Turks achieved almost complete surprise," Erickson writes, "as many as a thousand British and Irish soldiers were killed in a matter of minutes." When the attack halted, the New Zealand Brigade and the British Thirty-eighth Brigade had fallen back 500 meters, and the British Thirty-ninth Brigade and Twenty-ninth Indian Brigade (British Indian Army) had retreated a kilometer and a half.[41]

The British did counterattack. Their training methods, rigorously applied, produced quality soldiers, lions in combat even when led by donkeys, no matter the soldiers' origin, South Seas, South Asia, or a slum in east London. In one counterattack, Kemal and his aides found themselves surrounded by enemy infantry. Then something struck him in the chest. When Rusen Esref Undaydin asked about the incident in 1918, Kemal replied, "Yes, I saw a bullet hole in the right side of my jacket. The military officer next to me [Nuri Conker] said to me, 'Sir, you've been shot.' I thought that hearing this might have a bad effect on the morale of our soldiers. So I put my hand over his mouth. 'Be quiet,' I told him."[42]

Artillery shrapnel struck the right side of Kemal's chest, precisely where he carried his pocket watch. The watch shattered and Kemal suffered a minor wound. Kemal added, "Liman Pasha took the shattered remains of the watch as a souvenir after this battle, and in return he gave me his own watch, which bore his family's coat of arms."[43]

All told, between August 6 and 10, the Commonwealth would lose 25,000 men, the Turks around 20,000.[44] Bitter combat persisted along the Ariburnu-Anafartalar front. Casualty rates were horrid and the battles of August 21 exacted particularly enormous losses. Liman von Sanders wrote that between August 22 and 26 the Ottoman Fifth Army had to transport 26,000 wounded men to the rear.[45]

✠

A trio of recent historians drew these succinct conclusions:

> The Kemal-inspired counterattacks of 9 and 10 August had, in reality, settled the fate of the Allies' second offensive.... Hamilton and his generals kept battering away in the vain hope that some advantage might still be got. They launched another three major attacks around Suvla in August, none of which materially altered the front line.... The August offensive broke the spirit of the Allied armies. They had thrown everything they could muster at the Ottomans but the resistance had not collapsed and no major breakthroughs were achieved. The Ottomans too, were weary, and both sides entered a convalescence period rather like the slowdown in fighting after the massive May attacks.[46]

The Allies suffered a strategic blow when Bulgaria entered the war as a Central Power in September, which opened a supply route from Germany to Turkey. In exchange, the Ottomans gave the Bulgarians the town of Dimetoka in Thrace.[47] On December 20 the British withdrew from the Suvla Bay-Ariburnu beachhead. In January 1916 the allies evacuated Cape Helles. Kemal missed the retreats. He fell ill and he fell out with Liman von Sanders and took a medical leave dated December 5. Ottoman Fifth Corps commander Fevzi Cakmak replaced him. Feyzi would serve as Kemal's chief of the general staff during Turkey's War of Independence.

From initial invasion to final withdrawal, the battle lasted 259 days, nearly three-quarters of a year. But it affected decades of subsequent history. Gallipoli served as a military and political leadership laboratory for post–World War I and post-Ottoman Turkey. "A cadre of seasoned commanders emerged, who would go on to bedevil the British for the next three years in Palestine and Mesopotamia…in the Turkish War of Independence (1919–1922), the majority of the nationalist army's had served in command assignments on the peninsula. In fact, in that army led by Mustafa Kemal [in the War of Independence] except for Lieutenant General Nurettin Pasha, every senior army and corps commander had served personally with Kemal at Gallipoli."[48]

The Gallipoli campaign confirmed Kemal's military skill. Yet, clever forms of exile exist if political leaders wish to minimize the influence and potential challenge of a contentious hero. Kemal felt Enver had snubbed him in September when, on an inspection tour, he failed to visit Kemal's headquarters. He had offered his resignation but Liman von Sanders refused it and had tried to stop the Enver-Kemal feud. Enver finally visited Kemal on October 31, but by then Kemal was continually squabbling with the German general. Kemal escalated the dispute when he complained that the Ottomans definitely employed too many German officers. The December 5 medical leave provided an excuse, if not a cover story, for a senior officer divorce.[49]

Kemal sought a new command; the word in Constantinople, however, was that Colonel Kemal would be wise to obey orders. After cooling his heels, he was given Sixteenth Corps, its headquarters now in Edirne. He took command January 27, 1916, and on January 28, Kemal and his staff drove through Edirne, greeted by posters proclaiming "Long live Mustafa Kemal, the hero of Ariburnu and Anafartalar." His friend, Staff Major Izzettin, had arranged it. In the capital, however, the sultan, Enver, and Essad took the public kudos. The Fifty-seventh and the Twenty-seventh Regiments of the Ninth Division received deserved imperial commendations. In the capital, Kemal received no public recognition for his defense of the Ottoman Empire's western front.

On February 16, 1916, Russian forces took the Ottoman fortress of Erzurum in eastern Anatolia. Ottoman defenders retreated, avoiding encirclement but losing over 300 field guns. The czar's armies were on the verge of breaking into central Anatolia. The Ottoman's eastern front was crumbling.[50]

CHAPTER 9

Eastern Front, 1916, to Palestine, 1918

THE OTTOMANS HAD HELD THEIR WESTERN GATE AT GALLIPOLI. NOW massive Russian armies had stormed and captured their eastern bulwark of Erzurum.

In early 1916, Russian soldiers were exploiting the Ottoman Empire's military vulnerabilities and threatening to enter their heartland via the same classic invasion corridor the Seljuks used from Asia into Anatolia in the eleventh century. Mus fell to the Russians in February; Bitlis surrendered in March.

The Russian operations leveraged Ottoman neglect. While it raged, Gallipoli received the troops, supplies, and attention. The Ottoman Third Army, deployed along the Caucasus front, was short of soldiers and poorly supplied. The general staff believed that snow and freezing temperatures would impede Russian operations and ensure stability in the Caucasus through the winter.[1] The region also lacked rapid and reliable supply and transport links to western Anatolia and Thrace. Rail lines from Constantinople reached Ankara and Konya, a third of the way to the "Front of the Dead," the dour nickname for the central and southeastern Anatolia battle line.[2] In 1916 the rail connection via the city of Adana in south-central Anatolia was incomplete; moving troops meant debarking, marching to the next rail head, reloading, and then repeating the tedious routine. The Adana link had trouble enough supplying forces fighting in Mesopotamia, yet another problematic Ottoman front.

The Ottomans responded to the Russian offensive as quickly as their inadequate transportation network permitted. On March 1 Ismail Enver ordered the Second Army under Ahmet Izzet Pasha to move from Thrace to southeastern Anatolia to support the Third Army. He proposed a counterattack, using the two armies as pincers to trap the Russian bulge. Kemal's Sixteenth Corps received orders to move east on March 10.[3]

Kemal arrived at Second Army headquarters in Diyarbakir on March 27. On April 1 he was promoted to brigadier general; from now on he, too, was a pasha. "It was his last promotion in the World War," one biographer wrote, "and he achieved it on merit at age 35."[4] On April 16 Kemal established his corps' headquarters in the town of Silwan, east of Diyarbakir. Two days later the Russians attacked at the northern edge of the eastern front and took the port of Trabzon on the Black Sea.

Kemal's new command was disorganized and desperately short of artillery pieces. Troops coming from Thrace in the corps' Fifth and Eighth Divisions arrived fatigued; they needed rest before seeing action. The new arrivals were better off than the poorly clothed men in the depleted units scattered along the front, where typhus and dysentery plagued their encampments. Kemal "telegraphed Constantinople for arms, reinforcements, medical supplies, but was hardly surprised when he received no answer."[5] Tapping his own abundant supply of energy and confidence, he began preparing his Sixteenth Corps for offensive action.

The terrain in the Second Army operational area was everyone's enemy, whether Russian, Turk, or ethnic Kurd who might see both antagonists as foes. In southeastern Turkey high, barren mountains tower above tributaries of the Tigris and Euphrates. Chains of brown and black ridges formed of lava flows and tuffs divide plateaus and hard plains, some under cultivation, some fit for herding, and others dreadful, horse-killing wastelands of volcanic sand. The largest single terrain feature is Lake Van, a huge saline lake with no outlet. The Murat River, a tributary of the Euphrates, passes near Mus, north-west of Lake Van.[6] The Murat flows west for several hundred kilometers (at one point passing near the city of Bingol) until it reaches the Euphrates. Bitlis, southwest of Lake Van, is a mile above sea level; from mountains to the north the Bitlis River plunges into a gorge and divides a narrow valley before it eventually enters the Tigris. Mus is around eighty kilometers northwest of Bitlis and the massif between them is rock-ridden and harrowed.

As the Second Army's counterattack plan evolved, Kemal's corps took charge of the area south of the city of Bingol and southwest of the Bitlis-Mus line.[7]

On July 2, before the Second Army was able to complete its preparations, the Russians attacked toward the town of Bayburt (in northeastern Turkey, south of Trabzon) in the Third Army's zone. The follow-up attack of July 19 reached the Erzincan plain; on July 25 the city of Erzincan fell. These battles, called the Coruh Campaign, were a disaster for the Ottoman army. The Russians shattered Enver's northern pincer, leaving the Third Army defeated and disorganized. The Second Army's offensive would be a solo effort and would start farther west in Anatolia, as Russian forces nudged the Second Army back toward Diyarbakir and Bingol and pressed the Fifth Division in the Bitlis River valley. Refugees fled the towns of Mus, Bitlis, and

Van and poured into Diyarbakir. Second Army commander Ahmet Izzet ordered his force to counterattack on August 2. The immediate objective was Malazgirt, north of Lake Van. Ahmet Izzet must have seen his plan's weaknesses as his Second Army continued to receive new units who were not ready for combat. With the Third Army reeling, the Russians could shift their reserves to counter any Second Army successes.[8]

Kemal had spent July conducting a personal reconnaissance of his corps' front. The Russians' latest thrust had thrown the Fifth Division down the Bitlis valley. Now the czar's forces were maneuvering, attempting to trap the division. That situation demanded action. He concluded that his forces must "correct the Mus sector" as well. When the Second Army offensive commenced, his corps could retake both Mus and Bitlis and drive the Russians east and north. He returned to his headquarters at Silwan, addressed corps supply shortages, and ordered his divisions to prepare to attack. The Second Army offensive began with its northern Second and Third Corps attacking. Third Corps' Seventh Division was on the left flank of the Sixteenth Corps' Eighth Division, but given their wide sectors, division liaison along the corps' boundary was tenuous. The Sixteenth Corps expected the Seventh Division to attack east along the Murat River. With on-the-spot coordination, the Seventh and Eighth Divisions' flanks could mesh somewhere west and north of Mus.

Fifth Division operations in the valleys and ridges around Bitlis began August 4; Eighth Division lead elements crept forward prior to August 5, when the Sixteenth Corps' assaults began. They launched continuous attacks in both division sectors, denying the Russians the opportunity to rest and reinforce. Nuri Conker's Eighth Division left its assembly positions northeast of the town of Kulp and advanced northeast through the pass and over the mountains toward the Murat River. Once its lead left flank forces entered the Murat River plain, they swung east toward the Eighth

Division objective: Mus. The direct distance from Kulp to Mus is eighty kilometers, and in early August the division's regiments held forward positions sixty kilometers from Mus. Threading the pass, crossing the intervening mountains, and then swiveling to the east on the plain, however, meant foot soldiers and pack animals trekked at least twice that far. Although trenches arrested maneuvers at Gallipoli and on the western front, the drive on Mus was a fine example of what World War I leg-infantry divisions could achieve when mobile operations were possible. Crossing ridges and pouring down through a pass on an enemy position had been the ANZAC premise on April 25, 1915. While they had faced different tactical circumstances and greater troop densities, the operational concept—move quickly through and around enemy forces and seize a deep objective from the flank—was similar: win by maneuver and not by body count.

The Eighth Division entered Mus on August 7, 1916, as the Russians retreated across the Murat.

Bitlis, with its black gorge and rugged mountain river, presented a different kind of tactical and operational problem. Ottoman and Russian forces began the battle in closer proximity and the rough terrain limited space for large-scale flanking maneuvers. The fight would be close and vicious, yet Bitlis was a prize worth the struggle. Seizing Bitlis would force the Russians to retreat over the mountains, into the Lake Van basin, then withdraw around the great lake's western shoreline—if they were fortunate. Kemal may have bet the terrain north of Bitlis would kill as many retreating Russians as his infantry and artillery did in the town. After heavy combat, Bitlis fell to the Fifth Division on August 8.

Kemal's aide, Sukru Tezer, wrote that the Sixteenth Corps' forward headquarters was located in the Fifth Division sector. When the corps launched its attack, fighting erupted "all along the front and we kept the enemy on the defensive. We captured Bitlis on the third day of the corps' offensive. Real success had been achieved."

On August 8 an ecstatic Kemal telegraphed Ahmet Izzet in Diyarbakir:

Commander. Headquarters, Second Army:
   Our forces took Mus yesterday and Bitlis today. We continue to pursue the enemy.—Commander, XVIth Corps

Second Army headquarters greeted Kemal's report with excitement and delight. The people in the streets of Diyarbakir rejoiced at the news of the victory.

Ahmet Izzet responded:

Mustafa Kemal Pasha, XVIth Corps Commander:
   We thank you for your soldiers' timely performance at Bitlis and your brilliant service as commander. I offer my congratulations and thanks.

The Russians withdrew and finally formed a defensive line northeast of the Murat River. Corps operations continued until August 16, with the Fifth Division taking the town of Tatvan on Lake Van. The Russians, however, counterattacked along the boundary of the Third and Sixteenth Corps in late August, hammering the Third Corps' Fourteenth Division and pressing the Seventh. The Eighth and Seventh Ottoman divisions were separated by the Murat River. Faced with a crisis, the Second Army turned control of the Seventh over to Kemal. The Fourteenth Division, commanded by Kemal's old friend Ali Fuad (Cebesoy), was defending the Capakcur Pass leading to Bingol.

Ali Fuad would write after the war,

In the summer months of 1916 during the bloody war with the Russians we [Kemal and I] were not able to see each other. I was defending the pass...against a very powerful Russian force and my unit suffered a significant loss....Kemal took the Seventh Division from Mus and came to my aid. He attacked the enemy so forcefully. He saved me from very difficult and dangerous circumstances. We finally succeeded in clearing the pass of Russians. On one of those good days, near one of the highest mountain peaks [Kemal arrived]....I came up to him, clicked my boots together, and saluted him. He said to me, "Welcome, Ali Fuad." Then he suddenly hugged and kissed me. "I have noticed," Kemal said, "that the Second Army commander left you without supplies. Therefore I asked them to let me come help you. I could not wait for our commander's official orders so I decided to come and save you myself. And thank God, I have saved you."[9]

⊕

In September the Russians completely reversed Ottoman gains. The Second Army's total losses, in August and September were severe. Kemal's victories at Bitlis and Mus and his relief of the Fourteenth Division were the bright spots.

By October the front had stabilized, the intense combat and rugged terrain having sapped both sides. Winter was approaching, and this time the Russians lacked the soldiers and supplies to launch a major attack.

Kemal had earned yet higher command. Between August 4 and August 8, the Sixteenth Corps had simultaneously conducted two very different but successful offensives along a ninety-kilometer front. Terrain squeezed the Fifth Division; Bitlis was a mountain battle and a city fight. Nuri's Eighth Division fought a mobile battle that required long tactical-approach marches followed by concentration near the objectives—actions that indicate detailed thought and effort went into analyzing march routes, anticipating enemy reactions to friendly movements, and ensuring sufficient and timely supply by positioning supply trains to move quickly to support mobile columns. Planning such operations takes experience and applied foresight.

Eighth Division operations also demonstrated Kemal could trust subordinates to fight the battle without his immediate presence, a deferential trait that higher-level command requires. He knew Nuri's weaknesses and he knew his strengths. Nuri understood Kemal's goals. The right- and left-wing independent command structure that Kemal and Nuri had improvised at Derna in 1912 actually provided a template for the corps' extended August 1916 operation, with the Derna valley the reduced-scale equivalent of the Anatolian ridges separating Bitlis and Mus. Kemal proved he could successfully plan and lead large, complex combat operations on a wide front, while giving experienced subordinates the flexibility to make situation-driven decisions in order to achieve overall mission objectives.

As for higher command: Ottoman fortunes were ebbing. Kemal witnessed the palpable desperation and misery as he traveled the Second Army area. In his diary he wrote,

> 7 November: Immediately after crossing Batman bridge, we saw a man lying on the road. He appeared dead from hunger. Another two, between the bridge and our bivouac....After the bridge, two horses that have just died (men and horses are dying of hunger).

> 16 November: I inspected the hospitals in Bitlis and found them clean....the chief doctor reports that when the houses allocated to the hospital were cleaned, they found the heads of some ten to fifteen Muslim women. I went to the mosque called Serefiya. It's full of dead animals and rubbish. A ruin. I came across an orphan called Omer and took him along. When they saw this they brought me another three orphans. This time I contented myself with giving them money.

> 21 November: Told the ADC that Bitlis reminded me of the ruins of Pompeii....

> 22 November: For eight or nine hours...I chatted with my chief of staff on abolishing the veiling of women and improving our social life. 1. Educating capable mothers, knowledgeable about life. 2. Giving freedom to women. 3. Leading a common life with women will have a good effect on men's morals, thoughts, and feelings. There is an inborn tendency toward the attraction of mutual affection.[10]

Ottoman forces in the east were in disarray and on the edge of defeat. Ottoman soldiers were courageous; their higher-level command structure, however, was flawed. The Second and Third Armies had failed to coordinate their attacks and paid for this grievous mistake in loss of life and territory. The organizational problem required swift correction, for spring 1917 looked to be the foreboding season of decision on the Great War's eastern front. To improve army-to-army coordination and direct the next (and perhaps final) round with the Russians, the Ottomans created an army group headquarters, the Anatolian Army Group, for which Ahmet Izzet assumed command. The battle-proven Kemal took charge of the Second Army. He had earned it: "Kemal had performed brilliantly as a divisional and group commander at Gallipoli. His stellar performance in command of XVI Corps further marked him for high command."[11]

At some point the route to high command inevitably detours through the back alley of political intrigue; it always runs into the unexpected situation or evolving crisis requiring the flexible adaptation of personal and organizational leadership skills. The career path of great military commanders has always been more byzantine than meeting the great test of battlefield competency, though battle is the human horror which radically differentiates the military officer's calling from that of effective organizational administrators, skilled technical planners, and charismatic actors.

Kemal's erratic odyssey from December 1916 until 1918, when he took command of the Seventh Army on the collapsing Palestine front, exemplifies military talent's opaque, uncertain, and challenging route through the complex terrain of human psychology, human interactions, and human aspirations in conflict—in other words, the wicked hell of real people in a society at war. Democracies, to their functional benefit and moral credit, offer the talented more opportunities to prosper than kingships or their modern equivalent, dictatorships. But cabals, guilds, parties, media, and insider networks that filter information, push favored candidates, and stifle brilliant outsiders afflict democracies as well.[12]

❖

At his Second Army command, Kemal developed a close relationship with an outstanding subordinate, Colonel Inonu Ismet. Ismet was "the perfect south to Mustafa Kemal's north...obsessional, cautious, serious, dependent on the ideas of others," yet "better read than his commander."[13] He "was a capable and experienced staff officer; a slow little man; neat and wiry in build, with a small head and large hooked nose, somewhat deaf, and with the quiet, silent manner of the deaf." He was even-tempered, patient, and persistent.[14] A tough soldier, Ismet would go on to lead Turkish forces in the War of Independence battles and succeed Ataturk as president of the Turkish Republic.

Kemal and Ismet began planning a spring 1917 offensive. Then external forces intervened. In March 1917 the Bolshevik revolution struck Russia and the czar's armies fled. Russian internal politics accomplished what German and Turkish soldiers could not. The March miracle, however, was balanced by the Mesopotamia disaster: on March 11, 1917, Baghdad fell to British and Indian forces.

Other dazzling would-be miracles enchanted Ismail Enver. For months he had mulled over an expedition to secure Mecca and Medina in the Hejaz. Whether originally Enver's dream or a German idea, Enver became its prophet. In Enver's estimation Kemal should command it. Kemal declined, "saying that he favored evacuating all Ottoman forces from the Arabian heartland and concentrating on the defense of Syria, which formed a barrier to the British advance into Anatolia itself."[15] Kemal based his military recommendation on the facts. Political and cultural insight guided his decision to refuse the command: the Muslim general who lost Islam's holy cities would face a political death sentence and perhaps a personal one as well.

When Baghdad fell, Enver resolved to retake it. Kemal would command the Yildirim Army Group, an Ottoman-German strike force. It would march from Syria into Mesopotamia and seize Baghdad. Enver did not bother to consider the intervening terrain, or if he did, he saw it as paper space on a paper map, traversed by an order issued on paper. Mere physical existence could not possibly impede his dream. An army might utilize the Euphrates as a route to Baghdad, if it had river transports to ship supplies—which the Ottomans did not. Nor had they trains or railways—there was no hashed black line on the paper, not from Syria to Baghdad. Three hundred thousand camels might be just enough to support a strike through the desert—get the camels, get the camel drivers, pack the herd with the right supplies. But the merciless desert heat would invade and desiccate the soldiers. The Yildirim Army Group would face a slow death march over sand and volcanic rock, its ponderous columns harassed by British aircraft and Arab partisans.

Kemal took command of the Seventh Army in Syria "with one aim in mind," to prevent Enver's regional commander, German general Erich von Falkenhayn, "from attacking Baghdad and destroying Seventh Army in a grandiose gesture."[16] In Syria Kemal and Falkenhayn argued; Falkenhayn inspected the front—and shelved the plan.

Then Enver turned toward Suez and Egypt: the Seventh Army would attack through the Sinai. Now Kemal sent his criticisms straight to Enver, copying Mehmed Talat and Prime Minister Said Halim. Ismet helped him draft the critique. In it Kemal "complained that the bonds between the Ottoman government of the day and the Turkish people had been severed. He described the corruption of government officials, accusing them all of accepting bribes, and he detailed the breakdown of the administrative machinery, the courts of justice and the economy." He concluded that "if the war continues, the greatest danger we face is the possibility that the great dynasty of the sultans, rotten in all its parts, may collapse suddenly from within."[17] It seemed unthinkable, but the same thing happened in Louis XVI's France and in 1917 czarist Russia. As for his thoughts on the Germans: "We are losing our country, which is likely to become a German colony soon. For this purpose, General Falkenhayn is using the gold he brought from Germany and the blood of the last remaining Turkish sons from Anatolia. Leaving any corner of our country to the influence and administration of a foreigner would mean the complete abandonment of our sovereignty at a time when it is all about the defense of the motherland."[18]

When Enver's government predictably rejected his critique, Kemal resigned his command, returned to Constantinople, and took a room in the Pera Palas Hotel. The army placed him on three months of sick leave. Meanwhile the British, led by General Edmund Allenby, attacked in Sinai with their vastly superior forces and by Christmas 1917 seized Jerusalem. British prime minister David Lloyd George welcomed the gift.[19]

Kemal loose in Constantinople and critical of the government was a problem to Enver, who eased Kemal out of the capital by giving him a diplomatic mission to Germany. He was to accompany Crown Prince Mehmet Vahdettin, the future Sultan Mehmet VI, on a trip to meet Kaiser Wilhelm and to survey the western front. Perhaps a firsthand look at the German war machine would impress Kemal. As they prepared to leave, Vahdettin flattered Kemal with claims of admiration, specifically mentioning Gallipoli. Kemal, unimpressed with the prince because he refused to travel in his military uniform, changed his opinion of the royal heir. Some argue this was Kemal's own egotistical frailty and his ability to "overlook any deficiency in a declared admirer." But Kemal was also seeking political influence. He encouraged Vahdettin to exercise his authority; during their journey, he suggested the prince take command of the Fifth Army covering the Gallipoli Peninsula and he would be Vahdettin's chief of staff. Vahdettin, a "somnolent man with sloping shoulders," would prove to be risk adverse.[20]

As for Enver's German war machine: it lacked oil, had lost nuts, bolts, and armor plate. The facts on the western front did not require powerful binoculars. Germany was gambling on a new offensive. If that failed, it would confront imminent defeat.

Kemal returned to Constantinople and illness struck; his kidneys were inflamed, and he experienced excruciating pain. Ottoman doctors sent him to Vienna for examination and the Viennese recommended the cure at the spa at Carlsbad. He spent June and part of July 1918 resting, drinking mineral water, taking spa baths, eating chicken for dinner, and encountering firsthand the Austro-Hungarian Empire's flour shortage.[21] In July 1918, Sultan Mehmet V died and Vahdettin became Sultan Mehmet VI. Kemal's former commander, Ahmet Izzet, was advising the new sultan (and would briefly serve as his grand vizier). Kemal received a note requesting his presence in Constantinople.

Back in the capital and living in the Pera Palas, he had a cordial audience with the new sultan. When asked his views, he was frank. The audience ended, however, with the sultan telling him, "I have discussed with their excellencies Talat and Enver Pasha what needs to be done." Kemal was summoned again, after Friday prayers at the Yildiz Palace. Two German generals sat with Mehmet VI as the sultan told him that he would command an army in Syria. Kemal knew the force was a "moribund command." In a palace anteroom he encountered the "gloating Enver Pasha." Enver, using the sultan, had given him a hollow force ripe for defeat. "Bravo, I congratulate you. You have succeeded," Kemal said to Enver, barely swallowing his anger. Kemal knew Enver had given him an impossible task. When the front collapsed, Enver would blame him. His new command, the Seventh Army, was in terrible condition and sorely pressed by the British and Indian forces in Palestine.[22] Enver denied it, providing updated information.[23] Kemal left immediately by train. At least Falkenhayn was gone, pulled from command in favor of Liman von Sanders—though Liman von Sanders and Kemal had last parted on icy terms.

❖

The Liman von Sanders–Kemal combination, whatever the personal friction, had won at Gallipoli. It would not in Palestine and Syria.

Allenby's British and Indian divisions had the combat advantage in quality as well as quantity, and they were preparing to hit the Ottomans with a decisive offensive. T. E. Lawrence (also known as Lawrence of Arabia) and his Arab guerrillas provided the Commonwealth with a troublesome harassing force, but also an unparalleled propaganda and cultural warfare asset.

The British had promised the Arabs their freedom. Hussein, a descendant of the Prophet, and his Hashemite warriors from the Hejaz signed on, as did Abdul Azziz ibn Saud and his Wahabi firebrands from the interior Nejd. This Arab revolt from the southern desert trumped any cry of jihad issued by the Ottoman caliph in Constantinople and completely stymied the Ottomans' Islam unity movement.[24] Diplomats François Georges Picot and Sir Mark Sykes, however, had already made other less commendable arrangements for Arab lands, carving "zones of influence" in former Ottoman provinces, satrapies by any other imperial name.

Who was the bigger liar, the British or the Ottomans? CUP stalwart and Enver-triumvirate member Ahmet Cemal was in Syria, in contact with Hussein and Abdul Azziz, and attempting to manipulate them with religious proclamations and buy them with gold.[25] From the Arab perspective—particularly those who believed as Hussein did—Arabs were quite capable of running their own independent states and all powerful European states lied, whether led by Christians or Muslims. The Sykes-Picot's and the Ottoman imperialists' duplicitous legacies produced yet another long volume of dirty human history, which the twenty-first century (Iraq, Tunisia, and Egypt provide examples) is only beginning to address.

In August 1918 Kemal arrived in Syria, took command of the Seventh Army, and his quick survey verified the impossible circumstances. He did have two corps commanders he could trust: Ismet and Ali Fuad. Liman von Sanders (his force still called the Yildirim Army Group) wrote in his memoir, without a trace of animosity, "This splendid general, whom I knew from the Dardanelles Campaign, was greatly disappointed on his arrival by the small number and exhausted condition of his troops, the more as Enver had put the situation in a far too favorable light and had given him incorrect figures." The first thing Kemal did was post two newly arrived battalions "in the rear of his wholly unsupported front line." When the third battalion of this regiment arrived, it deserted. The British propaganda campaign describing the Ottomans' decrepit situation had reached them before they reached the front. "Among many other kinds of papers the British airplanes dropped wagonloads of the most beautifully illustrated pamphlets showing the physical comforts the Turkish soldier enjoyed in British captivity. The effect of such means on men who never got enough to eat and in many ways received no care of any kind should not be underestimated."[26]

The climate and terrain took their toll. "All hospitals and convalescent homes far to the rear were overcrowded," Liman von Sanders recalled.

> In the valley of the Jordan, where the heat frequently rose to 131–133 degrees Fahrenheit, troop movements between 8 A.M. and late afternoon were impossible. The Turkish soldiers had no summer clothes, but wore their cloth uniforms which might better be called rags. That the British and Indian dead left before the Turkish front were promptly robbed and found naked is not to be looked upon as intentional cruelty. It appeared to the Turkish soldiers the only means of procuring clothing, linen, or boots. All orders against the spoliation of the dead were in vain...it was perfectly clear to me that the ultimate decisive events were approaching.

Liman von Sanders claims he thought about a voluntary retirement.[27] Kemal had to have considered the prospect of retreat. A retreat would save the lives of Turkish soldiers for the future defense of Anatolia.

On September 11, 1918, Enver promised Liman von Sanders "all kinds of help for the Army Group, but none came in time."[28] The army group consisted of three weak armies: the Seventh commanded by Kemal, the Eighth by Jawad Cevat (deployed between the Seventh Army and the Mediterranean coast), and the Fourth in Syria, overseen by Ahmet Cemal, the CUP political kingpin and Syria's governor general. The Fourth Army had troops in the city of Amman and along the Jordan River, loosely covering the Seventh Army's left flank.

Allenby's remarkable plan of attack combined conceptual simplicity with calculated audacity. His army would start with a feint, strike with a sledgehammer, then unleash a terrible scythe. Massed Commonwealth infantry divisions backed by concentrated artillery—Allenby's sledgehammer—would smash the Ottomans' fortified line. Horse cavalry divisions—his scythe—would pour through this breach, bypass supporting Turkish positions, and then drive deep to attack rear area logistics depots that supplied the three Ottoman field armies.[29] Destruction of the supply dumps was not the only goal; psychological shock can also shatter combat forces. Mobile cavalry formations running rampant behind the Ottoman lines would sow confusion and incite fear, further demoralizing the already desperate Turkish soldiers. Allenby's plan specifically identified Nazareth (where Liman von Sanders had his headquarters) and Meggido as deep objectives for the cavalry units.[30]

Allenby decided the Ottoman Eighth Army line, which anchored its right flank on the Palestinian coast, was the prime spot to hit with his infantry's initial penetration attack. He implemented a shrewd deceptive operation to conceal this main effort. Commonwealth forces would first feint east toward the Jordan Valley (Kemal's inland sector), then concentrate on a very narrow front near the coast for the sledgehammer assault on the Eighth Army. After the breakthrough, Allenby envisioned a complex, mobile battle, one in which maneuver in the form of carefully planned flanking and encirclement operations—carried off with speed and discipline—would destroy the staggering Ottoman armies. Subsequent attacks would seize Damascus and Beirut, and ultimately southern Anatolia's ports such as Iskenderun.

Allenby's forces conducted the operation with veteran confidence and precision. At 4:30 A.M. on September 19, 1918, his reinforced corps attacked a twenty-kilometer-wide area along the Mediterranean coast. The Ottoman Eighth Army buckled and fractured as the British cavalry swept away through Turkish regiments. Haifa and Acre fell by September 25. One historian termed it "the swan song of the British cavalry," and a grand final aria it was—the British horse soldiers' last, massed dash-and-pursuit rates as one of history's greatest cavalry campaigns. The British would call the series of battles the Battle of Meggido; the Ottomans would call it the Battle of the Nablus Plain—a disaster that left them broken and defeated.[31]

To the east, Kemal's Seventh Army withdrew toward the Jordan River as British attacks hit its right flank. Kemal positioned rear guards to slow the pursuit and fell back with his main force. Establishing a coordinated defense was impossible. As his soldiers retreated, they passed Arab villagers dressed in festive clothes, "ready to welcome the enemy." Liman von Sanders considered defending Damascus, but his units that escaped the envelopment were too scattered. Kemal gathered the stragglers and told some trusted officers to reorganize the men into units. The British pressed on. With Ismet's corps near Damascus and Ali Fuad's in the Baalbek Valley, Kemal acted. Risking censure by Liman von Sanders, he exceeded his authority and ordered his forces to go north; Liman von Sanders, after conferring with Kemal, agreed with the orders. Ottoman forces would retreat to Aleppo in northern Syria, all but abandoning Palestine.[32]

Australian cavalry entered Damascus on October 1, 1918. Kemal's forces arrived in Aleppo on October 5. He placed two divisions south of the city. Ismet's corps continued north—Kemal knew Aleppo would become untenable and he was thinking of what came next.[33] During the retreat his kidney problem flared; the city's Armenian hospital and then his room in the Baron Hotel became his headquarters. British armored cars (Rolls Royce vehicles with turret-mounted machine guns) probed Ottoman defenses on the city's southern outskirts and boldly demanded surrender. They did not get it, but violence committed by Arab partisans wracked the city. Ottoman soldiers panicked. Street fighting raged. Kemal, "a slim blue-eyed assured figure, in impeccable uniform, with a cigarette between his lips" took control. As he "strolled down the street...he observed that certain inhabitants of Aleppo, whom he aspired to defend, were throwing grenades at him from the rooftops."[34] His troops were already moving out, heading north. On October 26 he shifted his headquarters to Katma on the edge of Anatolia. In the process, he had his rear guard strike a probing British unit north of Aleppo; it would be the Ottomans' last engagement, a bloody little punch on the southern slopes of Anatolia.

On October 30, 1918, the Ottoman Empire signed an armistice with the Allies. The ceremony took place aboard a British warship anchored in Mudros harbor off the island of Lemnos, hence the Mudros Armistice. The next day Kemal took command of Liman von Sanders's husk of an army group; in effect he now commanded Ottoman forces from Iskenderun to Iran, including those in northern Iraq.

The Ottoman Empire had lost. The victors would divide its provinces and attempt to shred Anatolia bit by bit. The army stretching from Iskenderun to Iran, however, was still a functional force, and it provided an armed boundary. A military force located somewhere in Anatolia, led by men with the will and wisdom to use it to defend the heartland, created possibilities the victors did not contemplate in their time of triumph.

Defeat into victory? Biographer Andrew Mango sums up the unique and strangely opportune moment well:

> Although largely unnoticed by the Allies, and still not well known in his own country [though Unaydin's articles were changing that], Mustafa Kemal had come out of the war in charge of the longest

front held by the Ottoman armed forces. He was only 37 and still a brigadier. But his professional reputation was high among Turkish commanders. True, they knew him as a difficult man to work with. He was ambitious and willful...played politics to get his way. He was convinced he knew best. But then he usually did, for he had good sense, a rare quality in a world that had torn itself to pieces.[35]

CHAPTER 10

Anatolia Surrounded

THE MUDROS ARMISTICE DID MORE THAN OPEN THE DARDANELLES AND Bosporus Straits to Allied shipping. Article 7 gave the victors "the right to occupy any points they deemed necessary for their security" throughout the entire Straits zone.[1] With the Narrows minefields diplomatically breached, Allied navies and armies moved to secure Constantinople.

Meanwhile, the defeated aristocracies of the Central Powers vanished. Kaiser Wilhelm abdicated November 9, 1918; a fragile German republic followed in his wake. Emperor Karl of Austria-Hungary abdicated November 13. Austria and Hungary became separate republics.[2]

The Hohenzollern and Habsburg emperors were gone. Though Western newspapers increasingly ran "Istanbul" as their dateline, and

"Turkish" usurped "Ottoman" as the prevailing description of his empire-less realm, the Osmanli sultan remained. Mehmet VI was still nominally the sovereign, albeit ruling a shrinking realm blighted by internal disorder and occupied by foreign armies. The British ran his capital, supplemented by a French contingent and augmented by conspiratorial Italian diplomats. Soldiers of the victorious Triple Entente barracked near the palace, stood guard around the Sublime Porte, smoked cigarettes and drank beer in the taverns. Their officers roomed in Pera's fine hotels and townhomes, lunched with Turkish notables at the best clubs and cafes, then telegraphed orders to Ottoman army units. Foreign naval cannon supported the soldiers' rifles with British, French, and even Greek warships anchored in the Sea of Marmara and off the entrance to the Bosporus. The Greek warships' iron presence fired passions, even among war-weary Turks. Everyone in the Balkans and Anatolia knew Greek ultranationalists, led by their prime minister, Eleftherios Venizelos, had vast territorial ambitions—the "Megali Idea." At Mudros, Rauf Orbay had begged the Allies to keep Greek forces away from the Straits and Anatolia. He argued that Greece had joined the Allied cause belatedly; that turmoil already afflicted the ethnically mixed communities of Anatolia's eastern Aegean seaboard; that the presence of Greek forces would incite, destabilize, and make the postwar occupation more difficult.

The Allies rejected the arguments. In 1917 they had used the prospect of territorial concessions in eastern Thrace and the Aegean littoral to coax the Greeks into joining the war. Britons educated at Oxford and Cambridge knew their Greek history, and it shaped their political perception. Izmir is simply a Turk mispronunciation of Smyrna, just as Istanbul is a mispronunciation of Constantinople, and Efes is Ephesus. Ephesians? St. Paul wrote epistles to Greeks, not Turks. Anatolian littoral? That's ancient Ionia. River Hermus to River Meander. Home of *Greek* philosophers, men shaping *Western* civilization, great chaps like Heraclitus of Ephesus.

Statements of republican sentiment roused the no-longer sedate Turkish coffeehouses in the capital and often became angry demands for *Turkish* nationalist action. The sultan and the occupiers also heard occasional calls for a "people's government," perhaps inspired by Bolsheviks, perhaps not. And rumored conspiracies filled volumes of Istanbul police and British intelligence files—nationalist conspiracies against the sultan; monarchist conspiracies to protect the sultan; military-led, foreign-linked, and foreign-controlled conspiracies to evict, assassinate, remove, or secure. This bazaar of intrigue and manifesto was the capital and the catastrophe to which Kemal returned in November 1918. That month the general staff disbanded his Yildirim Army Group. He asked for another—any—field command. Instead, he "was placed at the disposal of the war ministry and recalled to Istanbul."[3]

In the capital Kemal saw firsthand that Mehmet VI sought to ensure his own survival and that of his dynasty. His privileged dynasty came first, Turkey came second.

◆

The victors held the sultan in a military, political, and financial vise; he knew it, and an understanding evolved. They found Mehmet VI's titular authority to be a useful administrative tool as they occupied attractive swaths of Anatolia. With the sultan's blessings, the Thrace and Anatolian remnants of his state would function as "a semi-dependent colony."[4]

In late 1918 and early 1919 the victors partitioned Anatolia by occupation; they intended to make the partition official writ when the Treaty of Sèvres was signed in 1920. French forces occupied the Adana region and Cilicia (the southern coast, north of Syria), and they controlled several other seaports in addition to their condominium arrangement with the British in the Straits zone. The Italians seized parts of southwestern Anatolia, including Konya and Antalya; they also claimed Izmir, to the Greeks' chagrin.

As for Greek ambitions, the world appeared ready for the Megali Idea: the Great Greek State incorporating all southeastern European and Anatolian ethnic Greeks in one nation. War had savaged Greece's Balkan rivals. The Ottoman Empire suffered an enormous defeat. Bulgaria, which joined the Central Powers, had lost and paid dearly. Though nominally a victor, Serbia in 1918 was damaged and exhausted. Greece, however, had become an Entente ally at an advantageous moment. Now victory and Ottoman devastation provided the historic opportunity to liberate Anatolia's Greek communities from Turkish domination and forge "Greater Greece." The decade of revolts and war that began in 1821 finally led to the independence of peninsular Greece. The First Balkan War had returned Salonika and Western Thrace. Now the Great War offered Eastern Thrace and Anatolia's Aegean littoral or ancient Ionia as spoils. With luck, Constantinople and Cyprus would fall under Athens's sway, perhaps the Black Sea's Pontus as well.

Myth, history, and splendid personalities snarled with bitter grievance make the Megali Idea one of the world's more gripping ethno-nationalist narratives. A tale connecting Homer, Alexander the Great, and Saint Paul has star power. In Athens's streets and factories circa 1918, historical injustice and lost glory gave the story aggressive political traction. Ardent believers declared the perfect time had arrived to right the historical wrongs. In Phrygia (west central Anatolia), Alexander the Great had solved the riddle of the Gordian knot: he sliced the rope puzzle with his sword blade. Now a terrible swift sword would liberate Anatolia's imprisoned Greeks.

❖

Allied control officers, per armistice agreements and continuing negotiations, proceeded with the task of disarming and demobilizing the Ottoman Army. Removing rifle bolts and artillery breechblocks were favored methods of rendering weapons inoperable. The firing mechanisms would be boxed and shipped off for destruction. In spring

1919 Allied control officers became particularly interested in the forces commanded by two of Kemal's old friends and allies. Brigadier General Kazim Karabekir's Fifteenth Army Corps, headquartered in Erzurum, remained fully functional and in control of large weapons and supply depots, and Ali Fuad had a force based in Ankara.

British intelligence had gotten wind of attempts by national-ist officers to obstruct the control officers. From coastal cities like Trabzon and even Istanbul, weapons and ammunition had a way of ending up deep inside Anatolia where control officers were few. If a control officer operating in Karabekir's faraway command found a weapons cache and ordered it emptied and destroyed, the odds were good that his orders might be left on a desk or lost by a courier, and the process would have to start again. If a control officer succeeded in loading a train with illegal materiel, the train might depart the loading station but a few kilometers down the track would make an unsched-uled stop. Fifteenth Corps soldiers would then unload the precious war supplies. Removed rifle bolts and breechblocks reappeared in stockpiled rifles and artillery pieces.

◆

In Istanbul a deeply discontented Kemal took a room in the Pera Palas. Then he found a townhouse near the War College and that became his temporary headquarters. In carefully selected and pro-tected venues, nationalist officers met to discuss the sultan, the Allies, their policy options, and perhaps their own ambitions.

Rumors of political conspiracies became rumors of violent plots. Many were real. Old violence spawned investigations. Allied investi-gators accused former Ottoman officials of war crimes. In April 1919 a provincial district governor convicted of war crimes against the Armenians was hanged.[5]

Turkish nationalism stirred. Kemal contacted several former CUP moderates about "the possibility of forming a nationalist gov-ernment." Kemal sought support for a nationalist movement, perhaps one blessed by the sultan. However, Ali Fuad, who had returned to Istanbul with a case of malaria, wrote in his memoirs that in February 1919 "Kemal told him that if he were not dispatched to Anatolia on an official mission, he would join the commander in Anatolia whom he trusted most." Ali Fuad also claimed that he and Kemal discussed thwarting demobilization and keeping committed nationalists in military and civil service positions.[6]

Veteran combat commanders realized the Turkish nationalists faced another multifront war. Karabekir and Kemal would later clash over who had first foreseen war with the Greeks in the west and Armenian nationalists in the east. Historian Erik J. Zurcher acknowledges Karabekir's vital role in building an effective military resistance:

> In the earliest phase of the national resistance movement (1918–20) Käzim Karabekir was the key military figure in Anatolia, because his force was the only regular army of any size the nationalists had at their disposal. Käzim successfully sabotaged the demobilization of his troops and in the autumn of 1920 he used them to force the Armenian republic to recognize Turkish territorial claims and cede the provinces of Kars and Ardahan to Turkey. Thereafter attention shifted to the western front and Käzim's role gradually became less important.[7]

Karabekir's memoirs bitterly criticize Kemal, and understandably so, since Kemal politically purged him in 1927. Karabekir accused him of coming to Anatolia belatedly and of radicalizing the nationalist movement. These accusations may well be the truth from Karabekir's perspective. Zurcher describes Karabekir as a limited, vain, though honest man and "not a farsighted politician," and also suggests Kemal "played a very delicate game which was perhaps beyond the grasp of Karabekir," a game with short-term, interim, and long-term objectives which were military, political, and cultural.[8]

Biographer Andrew Mango favors Karabekir as the man who concluded that basing the resistance in eastern Anatolia was the best stratagem for the nationalists. This is very likely as his actions certainly indicate that he saw the possibility as the war ended. When Karabekir withdrew with his First Caucasian Corps from Persia and was retreating through the city of Batum, "he found Japanese field guns and ammunition in military stores and shipped them to Trabzon." But Mango also acknowledges the big picture: "Kemal, Rauf, Ali Fuad, Karabekir, and Refet (Bele) were the original military planners of the Turkish War of Independence." They knew each other and had served together during the war. Ali Fuad and Karabekir were related, and Karabekir and Ismet were close friends.[9] Given their relationship, Ali Fuad is more likely to have had insight on Kemal's political and military thinking as well as his plans.

✦

Kemal's personal opportunity came in the form of an appointment as inspector general of forces in eastern Anatolia.[10] The Ministry of War had begun reorganizing the army, and Kemal was on the short list for the position of inspector of the new Ninth Army in eastern Anatolia.

Kemal met two officials for lunch at the Cercle d'Orient club in Pera, where senior Ottoman officials as well as local Europeans and foreigners often dined. Then the war minister, Sakir Pasha, summoned him and confided that "his task as inspector would be to resolve Greek complaints of harassment." Pontus was experiencing incidents of ethnic friction, especially with the Greek government's vociferous demands in western Anatolia. Kemal received his commission as inspector April 30, and part of his charge was to see to the collection and safe storage of weapons. In addition, he was to investigate reports that the army was involved with local councils or possibly soviets in eastern Anatolia. When another army area inspector complained about Kemal's power, "the grand vizier replied that the sultan had taken the decision to test the ability of Mustafa Kemal with whom he had a special relationship of trust." Kemal assembled a "staff of fifteen officers and two cipher clerks."[11]

Before he left, however, the Greek army drew its sword and thrust its blade in Smyrna on May 15, 1919. Greeks and Turks shot it out, resulting in 300 to 400 Turks killed or wounded, and 100 Greeks, two of whom were soldiers.[12]

The exact circumstances of Kemal's departure from Istanbul remain in dispute. The cloak-and-dagger tale of a hunted man escaping the British snare is exciting; more likely, however, Mustafa Kemal Pasha was treated well since he was the sultan's representative. But the sultan's license does not negate the covert operation angle. His actions once he reached eastern Anatolia substantiate his claim that he "hoodwinked" the sultan and his current grand vizier, Damat Ferit,

On May 19, 1919, after three days aboard the steamer *Bandirma,* he landed at the Black Sea port of Samsun.

CHAPTER 11

The War of Independence

KEMAL'S LANDING AT SAMSUN IN MAY 1919 AND THE SIGNING OF THE Treaty of Lausanne in July 1923 serve as practical and symbolic markers for the beginning and the end of Turkey's War of Independence. Intellectual designs and physical capacities existed prior to May 1919, but Kemal's entrance into Anatolia began a political resistance movement that would create far greater physical capacities and fuse them into a dynamic, war-winning, political instrument. Grave internal conflicts and culture-changing political reforms followed well after mid-1923; however, the British, French, Italian, and Greek signatures on Lausanne's complex agreement certified an astonishing historical alteration had occurred, one with such sustaining force, clarity, and legitimacy that it could not be disputed, only affirmed.

On May 19, 1919, when he stepped onto the pier at Samsun, the obstacles Kemal's nascent independence movement confronted appeared overwhelming. Antagonists Great Britain, France, and Italy had crack military forces occupying Turkey's wealthiest and most productive regions. Armenian nationalist forces eyed eastern Anatolia, and "there were reports that 10,000 Armenian soldiers were massing at Kars and Sarakamis."[1] The Greek corps at Smyrna received regular reinforcements and sly encouragement from the Great Powers, especially the warmongering British devotees of Greek culture and history in London. The Megali Idea inspired the Greeks; they came to Smyrna to annex it. On the down side of this asymmetry, Kemal and his nationalist officers had the skeleton of an army, no money, and no diplomatic standing. The world recognized his sultan's government, but its sovereignty was a calculated charade.

The nationalists did have gritty personal courage, patriotic determination, a corps of men with guns in a strategically isolated territory, and Kemal's talents backed by his boundless energy and confidence. In May 1919 at the beginning, they also had an opportunity—one Kemal seized—to expand their moral influence among Turkish communities: the politically galvanizing effect of a Greek army in Smyrna. When organized and led judiciously yet opportunistically, and, most importantly, when vested with political legitimacy, these initial assets proved to be a powerful combination. Using these assets—human talent honed by war and suffering, fierce moral commitment, a geographic advantage, a functional military force, and visionary but adaptable leadership with superior communication skills—in four short years Kemal would lead a dispirited people from stark defeat in the Great War to a stunning military and diplomatic victory.

Kemal's military skill and insight, which were vital to the war effort, combined organically with his political endeavors, diplomatic operations, and media savvy. Promoting and shaping a new Turkish identity while building a new Turkish political entity were essential elements of his grand strategy. Yet he also set two concrete, uncompromising strategic objectives: preserve Anatolia and eastern Thrace as Turkish, and force all foreign troops to leave. Use of the telegraph as a rapid communications and coordination medium was a critical technical skill. Kemal also used the telegraph as a tool of personal influence; in the chaotic weeks following the Greek landing at Smyrna, he made himself a bold and articulate information and decision-making nexus for the nationalist movement. Taken in its entirety, the War of Independence demonstrated Kemal's genius for integrated and dynamic strategic operations, with victorious combat operations one component of his strategic success. To recall Qiao and Wang's analysis of gifted combinations, Kemal consciously combined "all of the means available at the time" to change "the tonality" of the conditions that existed at the end of World War I. He also began to address the conditions that had so fatally weakened and fossilized the Ottoman Empire.[2]

From their eastern Anatolian base the Turkish nationalists faced a multifront conflict against regular and partisan forces. Numerous small resistance groups existed in Anatolia, many that were little more than local militias providing security in a broken state incapable of ensuring police protection.[3] Others were fronts for bandits; a few had political designs and were but a step away from becoming insurgents. For Turks familiar with them, US president Woodrow Wilson's principles of self-determination (e.g., diplomats must consider a people's self-proclaimed interests in any just peace settlement) provided inspiration.[4] The groups lacked unity. For gang leaders hooked on plunder, genuine unification with a political movement and submission to its authority had little appeal. However, like the Greeks, Bulgars, and Albanians of Rumelia, these Turkish groups represented the beginnings of a mobilized people. Not all Anatolian militias were Turkish. Greek villages scattered throughout central and southeastern Anatolia had militias that were potential cadres for antinationalist guerrilla forces.

Kemal's reputation preceded him. Allied control officers watched him. British captain L. H. Hurst met Kemal in the town of Havza (eighty kilometers inland from Samsun). He departed "with the feeling that mischief was afoot." Kemal maintained telegraphic contact with army units in Anatolia, including forces near Izmir. Hurst reported that Kemal was "organizing a movement" which, in his opinion, would lead to massacres. On June 8 Kemal received a telegram from the Ministry of War which said "the British do not approve of your activities in that region...and have requested your recall." That same day, British High Commissioner Admiral Sir Somerset Gough Calthorpe cabled the Foreign Office: "It has come to my certain knowledge that various army officers have left Constantinople (Istanbul) with a view of organizing opposition to the Greeks. The movement is so natural, and I feel it so universal, that it seems to me hopeless to endeavor to stop it."[5] Calthorpe had identified the explosively central Turkish passion: the Greeks' landing at Smyrna. Reaction to the landings, especially among Turks with the slightest of nationalist leanings, was spontaneous; they were ready to resist. Calthorpe knew that the weeks following the landings were politically pivotal. So did Kemal. Hurst reported on June 12 that Kemal "had been carrying on a large telegraphic correspondence with the surrounding towns and beyond, so much as to have practically monopolized the telegraph...I am of the opinion that a definite movement against the Greeks is being organized."[6]

Since at least May 29 Kemal had been using the telegraph system to make himself the central node in an opposition network spread throughout Anatolia. He also exchanged views with the First Corps commander in Edirne (Thrace). On June 16 Ottoman interior minister Ali Kemal tried to disrupt Kemal's resistance and information warfare network by instructing "post offices [which handled telegraphic communications] throughout the country" to refuse to transmit or accept "protest telegrams."[7] Kemal responded by sending a telegram "on his own authority" threatening to court martial "any official who obeyed the interior minister's ban on the transmission of telegrams from resistance organizations." His slap back led to a compromise that permitted telegram transmission if "approved by local authorities." The compromise was a victory for Kemal. He would later say "that he had won the War of Independence by the use of telegraph wires."[8]

The telegraph-linked network of influence Kemal established likely played a major role in his own survival. In late June the Ministry of War proposed that Kazim Karabekir replace Kemal as inspector general; the British and now the minister of war wanted him out. The offer to Karabekir, the key military figure in Anatolia, was also a thinly disguised attempt to divide and conquer. Karabekir declined, though he was concerned about Kemal's contacts with Russian Bolsheviks. Kemal, however, assured Karabekir that he intended to play the Bolsheviks off against the Allies and use them as a source of weapons and money to continue his activities.

Some scholars divide the War of Independence into three phases: phase one was Toward a National Assembly (May 19, 1919, to April 23, 1920); phase two, the Grand National Assembly as Commander in Chief (April 23, 1920, to August 5, 1921); and phase three, Ataturk as Commander in Chief (August 5, 1921, to September 1922).[9]

The Amasya Circular, which Kemal wrote with advice from Ali Fuad and Rauf Orbay and with the approval of Karabekir, was a key document in the process of creating phase one, a nationalist congress. Issued June 21, it declared that Turkey needed a "national body free from outside control" and that a "national congress" would meet in the town of Sivas following "a congress of the eastern provinces" scheduled for July 10 in Erzurum.[10] The circular sketched Kemal's political plan.

Kemal knew Istanbul would eventually relieve him of his inspectorship; the Amasya Circular challenged the sultan's government. Refet Bele sent Kemal a telegram from Sivas, recommending that he resign his commission to avoid a charge of treason.[11] Kemal, knowing the Turkish people respected the authority of military officers, "wanted to use his title as long as possible." But few believed Kemal acted on behalf of the government. On July 7 in Erzurum (Karabir's headquarters) he issued one final telegraphic circular, telling military commanders to retain weapons, support national organizations, and that "there should be a united military response to any further movement of enemy troops." That point stuck; the sultan would not or could not do anything about the Greek army in Anatolia. On July 8, in the midst of a telegraphic debate with the minister of war, Kemal resigned his military commission. However, when one of his subordinates left him to seek an appointment with Karabekir, Kemal's confidence plummeted.

In his October 1927 speech, Kemal said he subsequently held a meeting, which Rauf, Karabekir, and several regional governors attended. He "argued that the national struggle should be waged by people fully prepared to take the consequences." The leader did not have to be him, but the movement needed a leader. "When the group reassembled…all present promised to support him." Rauf disputed Kemal's version, though not its essential conclusion. Rauf wrote that Kemal agonized over his resignation, insisting it was a mistake. Karabekir came to Kemal and said, "You remain our respected commander, just as you've been until now.... Pasha, we're all at your service."[12]

Kemal's military reputation counted. Although his confidence may well have slid after his resignation, his moments of despair were fleeting. Karabekir was a competent soldier who could hold eastern Anatolia, and at conscious and unconscious levels, he knew the nationalist cause could not flourish without Kemal. In terms of asserting Turkish interests, compared to Karabekir, Kemal had a global reach and grasp, the communications skills, and a clearer grasp of politics.[13] He would direct the congress at Erzurum in July and then convene the Sivas congress in early September.

The two congresses advanced the process of building an open national resistance movement and establishing its political legitimacy.

At Sivas the nationalists made strides toward forging a common front. April 1920 would see the Grand National Assembly seated in Ankara.

Quarrels with Istanbul persisted, and Kemal spurred them, for the rhetorical jousts sharpened differences and enhanced nationalist stature. It is a classic technique, "arguing up," and Kemal used it deftly. He repeatedly accused Istanbul of failing to protect Turkish interests. He occasionally made superficially conciliatory gestures, such as offering to cooperate with the government if it agreed to support Turkish independence. The nationalists demanded that delegates to the upcoming Sèvres peace conference should be "people enjoying the nation's confidence," meaning Turkish nationalists. This delicious poke of course implied the people lacked confidence in the government.[14]

A French move in late October 1919 interrupted the rhetorical duel. French troops replaced British soldiers in Marash in southern Anatolia. Armenian militiamen and Armenian refugees returning to their homes in the area accompanied the French. Ethnic warfare erupted between Turks and Armenians. Kemal responded by supporting Turkish guerrillas in the region. Given the presumed power of the French forces and the nationalists' military weakness, insurgency was, for the moment, the only realistic option. French diplomats, however, saw the response and feared an alliance between Turk and Arab nationalists as the French intended to solidify their position in Syria. Georges Picot (of the Sykes-Picot Agreement, which split Ottoman Middle Eastern domains between France and Britain) visited Kemal in Sivas in December. Picot wanted a deal. Kemal agreed to stop Turkish attacks if the French and Armenians did likewise. Given the militia chaos, the attacks did not stop, and a halt was not in the nationalists' interests. They were at war with the occupiers. Kemal correctly interpreted Picot's visit as an exploitable crack in the Allied political front. France might ultimately support Turkish nationalist goals. Serious fighting hit Marash in late January 1920, which some observers characterized as a Turkish rebellion while French and Armenian sources saw it as a nationalist attack since a small force of regular Turkish soldiers aided the guerrilla action. The combat's political message—we will fight an Allied power—far outweighed its military significance. By early February, weak nationalist forces held Marash and Urfa.

The British, however, reacted vigorously. If their allies could not control Anatolia, they would exercise their control in the capital and pressure the Ottoman government. In mid-March 1920 British forces occupied Ottoman government buildings in Istanbul and arrested nationalist leaders. Kemal sent telegrams urging the nationalists to protect "the safety of non-Muslims" and avoid ethnic and religious reprisals. He also declared that the British occupation of government chambers ended "the seven-hundred-year-old Ottoman state."[15]

The British action left Kemal's now Anakara-based movement the unrivaled center of nationalist resistance. In May, nationalist forces skirmished with the French in Cilicia, and Turkish partisans captured 500 French soldiers.[16]

On August 10, 1920, the Treaty of Sèvres officially partitioned the Ottoman Empire. Sultan Mehmet VI and Grand Vizier Damit Ferit endorsed it. Armenia received significant territory in the east. The nationalists reacted on the battlefield. Karabekir's soldiers occupied Sarkamis in September 1920, took Kars on October 30, then threw Armenian forces beyond the Arpacay River. Armenian and nationalist officers signed an armistice on December 2, which fixed the Armenian-Turkish border. Karabekir's offensive secured the east and revealed that the Allied powers could not enforce Sèvres without a massive military commitment.[17]

Greece, however, posed the greatest military and political challenge. By any reasonable standard, the Treaty of Sèvres was a Greek territorial triumph. Greece received the Dodecanese Islands (except Rhodes) and all but a sliver of Thrace. After an interim of five years, Greece would gain full control of Smyrna and a substantial slice of its Ionian hinterland.[18] By mid-September Greek forces had occupied eastern Thrace and in Anatolia advanced to the Bursa-Alashehir line. In October Turkish partisans attacked a Greek unit in Gediz (east of Smyrna) and suffered heavy casualties.[19] Greek forces in Bursa attacked eastward. For several months Prime Minister Eletherios Venizelos's Greek government had sought Allied permission to attack and destroy the nationalist forces, if it could not gain their help. The Entente allies lacked the will, though "nothing less would reduce the Kemalists to impotence."[20] Venizelos lost the November 1920 Greek elections, held just after the death of young King Alexander. (A monkey had bitten Alexander as he strolled his palace gardens, and the bite killed him.) The new government, despite openly discussing withdrawing its army, finally committed itself to seeking military victory in Ionia.[21] In early January 1921 Greek forces probed Turkish lines, then withdrew, calling it a reconnaissance in force. Kemal claimed a victory, the First Battle of Inonu;[22] he exaggerated, but in war, hyperbole is a weapon usually wielded by the weaker side, and nationalist morale needed a victory. Greek diplomats realized Kemal and his Kemalists (the word gained cachet) would never accept Sèvres. They had convinced themselves they had popular support, that Anatolian peasants would welcome them as liberators, because the Nationalists imposed stiff war taxes.[23]

In October 1920 the Venizelos government had informed Britain it would pursue a military solution, had requested money and war materials, and brazenly suggested that British troops in Anatolia cover the Sakarya River as the Greek army advanced. The new government sacked several of its predecessor's military officers but continued planning for an offensive. At the London Conference of February 1921 (with a delegation of Kemal's nationalists in attendance) the Greek delegation claimed, "The Greek Army in Asia Minor, 121,000 strong, is in position to scatter the Kemalist forces and to impose the will of the Powers as embodied in the Treaty of Sèvres." The British disagreed with Greek assessments of the Nationalist (now a capital N) military capacity. The Turkish Nationalist delegation, hoeing the hardline, demanded the evacuation of all Greek forces.[24]

The Greeks attacked March 23, 1921, on two fronts, its Southern Group from Ushak to Afyon Karahisar and its Northern Group marching from Bursa. The Nationalists now had a substantial force of regular troops, and another battle developed near Inonu in which a furious Greek bayonet charge broke the Turkish line. The Nationalist army, led by Ismet, counterattacked, and the Northern Group retreated, then withdrew to Bursa. It was reported in the *Manchester Guardian* that "the [Greek] men were angry—angry at spending so much blood and labor in vain, but even more humiliated at a defeat which broke a long record of victory."[25]

Kemal telegraphed Ismet with words intended to encourage the Grand National Assembly in particular and every Turkish nationalist in general: "Few commanders in the whole history of the world have faced a task as difficult as that which you undertook in the pitched battles of Inonu.... It was not only the enemy you have defeated, but fate itself—the ill-starred fate of our nation." The Nationalists, however, lost 5,000 dead at Inonu, and another 2,000 deserted, but the battle stopped the Greek advance.[26]

On the diplomatic front, alliance cracks had become wide fissures. France and Italy told Nationalist diplomats they would accede to Turkish territorial demands if guaranteed economic advantages in the territories. Kemal did not present the proposals to the Grand National Assembly. He foresaw a battlefield victory that would create such favorable strategic conditions, no concessions would be required.[27]

In July the Greeks launched an offensive aimed at Ankara. They intended to destroy the Nationalist's regular army, occupy Ankara, and either kill or capture their leadership. On July 10, the Greek army hit the railway line linking Eskishehir and Afyon Karahisar as forces in the south attacked. Kutahya fell July 17 and Eskishehir July 19. Kemal himself ordered the army to retreat, saving Ismet the stigma.

"Kemal had recognized in ordering retreat, the further Greek forces were drawn from their bases, the more difficult and dangerous would be the attempt to annihilate the Turkish army." This sound military decision, however, entailed political risks. "Mustapha Kemal had staked his political existence on the unpopular policy of controlled withdrawal—a policy which required iron strength and confidence to draw the Greek army into not a trap but a wasteland where it would destroy itself."[28]

The Nationalist army made their stand at the right time and in the right place. Kemal maintained the most suitable place to defend was north of the Sakarya River.

He issued a directive, under the authority of the Grand National Assembly: "After the army has been concentrated north and south of Eskishehir, we must establish a large area between it and the enemy's forces, so that we shall be able to carry on our reconstitution, reorganization, and reinforcement. For this purpose we should be able to retire even to the north of the Sakarya. If the enemy should pursue us without coming to a halt, he would be getting farther away from his base of operations. Thus our army will be able to rally and meet the enemy under more favorable conditions."[29]

Kemal led with his binoculars and map. The Sakarya River swings east across the Anatolian plateau, then north, then west. Its banks are steep, and in 1921 there were few bridges. In effect, fifty miles west of Ankara the river creates a large loop of terrain of barren ridges.[30] Within this arc and to the north of the Great Anatolian Salt Desert, the Nationalists built a defensive line of some one hundred kilometers. It consisted of strong points backed by mobile reserves.

Rauf Orbay would recall, "The Greek armies were marching on to Ankara. Early in the morning we met at the National Assembly. We were going to be informed by him. He [Kemal] asked for a map of Anatolia, we brought it. With a red pen he drew a broad long line in the rear of Sakarya and pointing to this line he said, 'We shall beat the enemy here.' We believed him, why and how we believed, I still don't know."[31]

The Greek army followed Kemal's systematic withdrawal. Kemal knew his enemy and he also knew his own side. Facing imminent defeat, "many [Assembly] deputies now turned to Kemal for salvation, urging him to assume full responsibility for the dire situation." Kemal would accept the responsibility, but in return he demanded to be fully empowered to take decisive action. He asked the Assembly to grant him "extraordinary powers" to serve as both Grand National Assembly president and supreme military commander. Political and military power must be seamlessly combined, he argued, because "in this most critical hour Turkish soldiers needed a single commander who possessed freedom to act quickly and decisively without the restraints of parliamentary debate." He got the authority, with a time constraint on what amounted to near-dictatorial powers. On August 5 the Assembly passed Law 144 making Kemal commander in chief of the Turkish Armed Forces for a period of three months.[32]

On August 14, 1921, the Greeks moved east. Three Greek corps, each composed of three divisions, advanced rapidly in an extended maneuver to outflank the Turks' positions and avoid frontal assault. They marched nine days before reaching Turkish positions near the Gok River. One marched through the desert, beneath the August sun. The Greeks' supply tether lengthened and strained; Greek logisticians had to lug water to the units on trucks.[33]

On August 26 an exhausted Greek army attacked the first line of Turkish defenses. By September 2 they had seized Chal Dag, the heights south of the Eskishehir railroad, and had advanced through the Turks' second defensive line. Kemal expected penetrations and actually permitted them. He had organized his army to fight a mobile defense within an area instead of along a specific, continuous trench line. The Turks had built a zone of fortified strong points, typically located on high ground to cover critical terrain. Reserve infantry units positioned to respond quickly to Greek forays supported the strong points. When Greek assault units attacked the first string of fortifications or slipped between them and plunged forward to hit another nest of bunkers and defensive works, the Turkish reserves would make tactical counterattacks. This mobile defensive scheme ultimately robbed the Greeks of the offensive initiative, for the Greek forces in the penetration confronted more strong points on the ridge before them and Turkish counterattackers on their vulnerable flanks. Instead of achieving a breakthrough they faced entrapment. To protect their gain and avoid encirclement, the Greeks would have to use their reserves to reinforce the shoulders of the penetration. That would take more time, more manpower, and more ammunition. The Greeks, however, were running out of time and supplies. To critics of his plan who perhaps found comfort in continuous trenches, Kemal explained his defensive strategy: "'There is no line of defense but an area of defense. That area is defense of the motherland.' This concept rested on flexibility of response and rapidity of movement, not a rigidity of positional warfare."[34] Kemal calculated that the Greeks would exhaust themselves in the morass of strong points and constant counterattacks and never manage a decisive breakthrough. Once they were exhausted, physically and mentally, the Turks would launch their own large-scale counteroffensive.

That massive Turkish counterattack began September 8 and continued through September 11, the day the Greek Army began to withdraw. Greek units left Chal Dag that night. On September 14 they crossed the Sakarya, heading back to Eskishehir where they had been a month earlier. They suffered 20,000 casualties in the Battle of Sakarya. As they retreated, they destroyed everything of value.[35]

Rauf credited Kemal: "He took this duty and vanquished the enemy at the line he drew. He returned from Sakarya to Ankara with a childish smile. By his personal effort, he had won a battle, which would have been the absolute end of the Turkish independency, if he had lost it."[36] The Turkish position had dramatically improved. Kemal's force received weapons and ammunition from Russian Bolsheviks.

British intelligence, however, had correctly concluded that Kemal and his government were "suspicious of Bolshevik agents and designs."[37] The British also believed that the Kemalists might negotiate an end to the war but would demand Greek evacuation of the territories they had occupied.

The lines along the Sakarya froze in place, but not the armies. The Nationalists grew in strength, while climate, terrain, and political doubt ate away at the Greeks. France reached a peace agreement with the Nationalists on October 20. Kemal had split the Allies. By spring 1922 Britain saw Greek evacuation as part of a potential general Near Eastern settlement. France, Britain, and Italy proposed an armistice. The Greeks accepted it, albeit awkwardly; the Turks did not. The proposal, unveiled March 26, recognized Turkish "'sovereignty in Anatolia' but made no commitments regarding the protection of 'Christian populations' (Greeks) in the region. Decisions regarding their security, the diplomats said, would be made by the Turkish nationalists after the Greek withdrawal."[38]

Greek army morale sank. By summer 1922 the Greek forces seemed on the verge of disintegration. Greek and Turkish forces on the south flank faced one another across the Meander River, Ionia's traditional boundary, where "Kemalist Turkish private soldiers brought eggs, cheese, and fruit" to the Greek soldiers in return for cigarettes.[39]

August 1922 found Greek forces basically in their July 1921 positions: Kios on the Sea of Marmara, southeast toward Eskishehir to Afyon Karahisar, then west down the Meander to the Aegean. Ten Greek divisions held the front; reserve forces were minimal. The time had arrived for the coup de grace. Kemal's forces now had Austrian- and German-made artillery on the ground and a squadron of French-manufactured airplanes overhead. Fourteen Turkish infantry divisions and four cavalry divisions concentrated in the southern sector near Afyon Karahisar, between Akar Tsai and Tulu Pinar.[40]

Kemal framed his plan succinctly: hold the Greeks in the center with Turkish II Army as the Turkish I Army attacks to the south. He took personal command of the battle along the Sakarya. His departure for the front was "shrouded in the utmost secrecy.... The papers announced that he had given tea to his mother. In fact, he had left Ankara by night and driven by car across the salt desert to the front."[41] He covered the attack with a diplomatic shroud. Kemal transferred "at night without detection a large part of his army from the north to the south while on the diplomatic front he made overtures suggesting a new willingness to negotiate a peace."[42]

"As zero hour approached Kemal issued a battle order to the troops, which had been drafted by Ismet. It read: 'Soldiers your goal is the Mediterranean.'" The Greek expeditionary army planned a battle of annihilation; now Kemal turned the tables. Before sunrise on August 26, Kemal moved his headquarters to a hilltop (Koja Tepe) with superb observation of a critical battle sector; he would direct the initial assault himself.[43] The Turkish artillery barrage began the Great Offensive, then Kemal's infantry struck along a forty-kilometer front as cavalry slipped through the gaps to cut rail and communication links. Having learned from a talented opponent, Kemal consolidated cavalry operations, emulating Allenby's 1918 Palestine offensive. Like Allenby, Kemal utilized a heavy sledgehammer to crack the enemy line and "achieved a five to one superiority" at the decisive point. The Fifth Cavalry Corps, Kemal's scythe of horsemen, was "positioned to strike deep."[44] The Greeks began withdrawing as Turkish cavalry penetrated their lines. They evacuated Afyon Karahisar on August 28. The Turks raced for the valley town of Dumlupinar, west of Afyon Karahisar, where on August 30 they surprised and shattered Greek forces withdrawing along the rail line. The decimated Greek regiments fled toward Smyrna.[45]

✦

When the news of their army's defeat reached Smyrna, Greek civil and military authorities abandoned the city. By September 7 thousands lined the waterfront, begging for space on a ship to Greece, to anywhere. Two days later, 400 Turkish cavalrymen arrived. That evening sporadic looting and killing began in the city, followed by chaos, revenge, hatred, and fear. On September 13 a fire erupted in the Armenian quarter, which by evening engulfed the town. The fire spared Smyrna's Turkish and Jewish quarters. The seaport's Armenian and Greek neighborhoods, however, became a pitiful wasteland of embers, ash, and blackened stones.[46]

Greece and Turkey signed an armistice on October 11, 1922, in Mudanya, a sleepy port on the Sea of Marmara near the city of Bursa.

In 1923, as the ink dried on the Treaty of Lausanne (which confirmed the Turks' victory) and historians scanned its 143 articles, for the first time in roughly two centuries a Turkish state could answer the question "What went right?" with a long list of positive results.

❖

In Kemal's October 1927 speech he said, "To speak of war means not only two armies but [in essence] two nations coming face to face and fighting against one another with all their being and all their resources, involving both material and spiritual resources. For this reason, I had to interest the whole Turkish nation in thought, sentiment, and action in the same way as the army on the front."[47]

Military analyst George Gawrych compares Kemal's analysis to Clausewitz's "trinity" of war, which is often popularly expressed as the people, the government, and the army.[48] "In essence, Kemal ranked the nation (*millet*), the constituent assembly (*meclis*), and the army (*ordu*) in order of ascending importance for the successful execution of the war, all organically linked in a sacred trinity. Parliament [the National Assembly], in addition to mobilizing the nation for the war effort, served as an effective means for presenting a united national front to the international community in future peace negotiations."[49]

In 1927, five years after the war ended in a Greek disaster and four years after the Treaty of Lausanne, Arnold Toynbee and Kenneth

Kirkwood wrote, with polished astonishment, "And the world had the unprecedented surprise of seeing a defeated and apparently shattered nation rise from its ruins, face the greatest nations of the world on terms of absolute equality, and win from the humiliated victors of the Great War almost every one of its national demands."[50] In Toynbee's estimate, Turkey's victory in the War of Independence, followed by Kemal's political and cultural revolution, reflected a global process, one he saw underway in China, Japan, Iran, the Arab Middle East, and especially in India. At that time Japan, which had made its revolutionary break during the Meiji Restoration, appeared to be the most successful example of rapid modernization. The new Republic of Turkey, with Mustafa Kemal as its leader, had made astounding strides.

Gawrych sees Turkey's War of Independence "as an early example in the twentieth century of a quasi-insurgency movement brilliantly executed to attain final victory." Subsequent twentieth-century independence and nationalist movements (e.g., Algeria) copied his methods. Gawrych argues that "Ataturk deserves recognition in the West as one of the great military strategists and commanders of the twentieth century, a soldier who understood well the relationship between politics and war, between national will and military power, and between strategy and tactics."[51] Ataturk swore he was born to be a soldier, and indeed he proved to be one of the twentieth century's best. Yet, his genius is, as Gawrych notes, for the most part unappreciated in the West and certainly in the Western popular press. That may be changing. World War I's centennial promotes reassessment and broader perspectives. The global terror war waged by militant Islamist factions like al-Qaeda have renewed interest in Ataturk's social and political reforms, which Ataturk viewed as political operations to reinforce Turkey's military victory. In the hindsight of one hundred years and the foresight of the next fifty, Ataturk is a twentieth-century leader whose strategic military and political achievements still matter.

CHAPTER 12

Ataturk at War in the Twenty-First Century

"I need you for what comes next."

—*Mustafa Kemal*

WITHIN DAYS OF THE MUDANYA ARMISTICE, KEMAL AND HIS GENERALS gathered in the nearby city of Bursa. Freed from Greek occupation in September, the city pulsed with postwar elation, relief, and anticipation.

One evening an eager crowd of citizens gathered in a Bursa movie house. And they were citizens now, Kemal told the Turkish citizens, not Ottoman subjects. Citizens bear responsibilities that subjects do not; freedom has burdens; free citizens must square the circle that freedom is not free, and uncertainty and imperfect outcomes always bedevil their struggle. Securing and maintaining political freedom requires a citizenry with economic skills, intellectual and social creativity, and the confidence to participate in the public process. With these energies channeled through political institutions that encourage them, uncertainty becomes an opportunity for renewal. And that is freedom's great social and personal good—the opportunity for renewal.

The old certainties had failed the Ottoman Empire. The old certainties of sultan and caliph took their army to the gates of Vienna but restricted creative debate and economic experimentation. The Ottoman assumption of cultural and theological superiority led to intellectual fossilization which stifled social innovation and cultural adaptation. Then came the flood of new ideas, compelling, productive ideas, primarily but not solely from Europe, whose empirical success challenged the old certainties' claims of God-ordained perfection. The railroad connected beautiful Salonika to the European system; the telegraph connected eastern Anatolia to the world. These were the physical manifestations of an increasingly interconnected globe that challenged the old certainties and revealed their material, social, psychological, and even spiritual frailties.

But the habits of centuries fade slowly. A sultan decided and decreed, his subjects accepted and toiled. The sultan's chains provided a type of psychological and social security that freed them from responsibility; the centuries of tyrannical chains had scarred the Turkish spirit. These figurative scars represented embedded moral forces more resilient than any enemy army. Kemal's struggle for Turkish cultural renewal had just begun.

On the stage in Bursa, with his officers seated, Kemal, the successful general and commander in chief, wore civilian clothes as he spoke, not a uniform. To secure our independence, he told the citizens, requires progress in economics, in education, and in political rights. There were many women in the audience, and he could see their faces. The Great War had put Turkish women into the workforce.

With men in the trenches, the women manufactured uniforms and sandbags. "Although the veil was still worn...many women no longer covered their faces."[1]

He had contemplated it, discussing the subject amid war's frenzy and desperation. Now he openly advocated freeing women politically in this poor, agrarian, culturally Muslim, and feudal society: "If henceforward the women do not share in the social life of the nation, we shall never attain our full development, incapable of treating on equal terms with the civilizations of the West."[2] He would say it again, to the Grand National Assembly, to the entire nation: "One of the necessities of today is to ensure the rise of our women in every way. Therefore our women will be scholars and scientists, and go through all the degrees of education the men do." Why? "If a social organization is content to meet contemporary requirements with only one of the two sexes, that social organization loses more than half its strength." Because "our women, like us, are intelligent and intellectual human beings....Let them show their faces to the world, and let their eyes look on the world carefully, there is nothing to be feared in this."[3]

Kemal insisted on political freedom for women in the 1920s. Modernity, Kemal's "contemporary requirements," demanded it. The idea of emancipating women still appalls many twenty-first century militant Islamists.

Kemal, the gifted strategist, argued that modernity required creativity and economic vitality. A creative and productive people needed education. In a speech given to a teachers' conference (also held in Bursa after the War of Independence), Kemal connected his battlefield successes to larger strategic and cultural goals: "The victories won by our armies have prepared the ground where real victories will be won in the field of education."[4] He also advocated a "unified education system" with "secular, Turkish-language schools."[5]

Kemal linked education to language reform and economic vitality. Perhaps 10 percent of Turkey's population in 1923 was literate.

This deplorable record made Kemal's proposal to Latinize the Turkish script more palatable, since the illiterate had no investment in the Arab-Persian script. Reformers had promoted the idea for decades, and the Young Turks had advocated Latinization of the alphabet because they believed it would ease trade and commerce.[6]

His speech to Turkey's Izmir Economic Congress on February 17, 1923, sketched national economic goals in practical terms, aided by pointed historical references, clever poetic imagery, and faith in the Turkish people's ability to achieve them

> Ottoman history is not a history of events and efforts carried out in fulfillment of the desires and requirements of the nation, but it is a history of events carried out in order to satisfy the personal whims and ambitions of a few despots.... An offer of a trade agreement with Venice was refused by Sultan Suleiman the Magnificent on the grounds it was incompatible with his honor.... Conquerors by the sword are in the end to be defeated by conquerors of the plow.... No matter how brilliant military victories and diplomatic achievements may have been, if they are not reinforced by economic achievements, they cannot be expected to last long. We have, therefore, to crown our brilliant victories with economic victories.[7]

Kemal's new battlefield was the future. In his visionary binoculars, plowshares bested swords.

✛

Cultural reform to promote continuous renewal moves beyond strategic warfare, which Kemal waged brilliantly, and enters the realm of long-term struggle, which is a form of conflict at the level of grand strategy. In this realm, where wicked social and psychological energy fields mix, wax, and wane, bullets are less important than beliefs.

On November 1, 1922, Sultan Mehmet VI left Istanbul for exile. The sultanate ended, though an Osmanli aristocrat remained in the capital. Crown Prince Abdül Mejid II, Mehmet's cousin, became caliph. In March 1924 parliament passed a bill which "deposed the caliph, abolished the institution of the caliphate, and exiled from Turkey all members of the Ottoman dynasty." At midnight on March 4, 1924, the last caliph left the Catalca railway station in a special coach car attached to the Orient Express. He died in Paris in 1944.[8]

The struggle to reform continues. In the twenty-first century militant political Islamists wage a global war to revive the caliphate, or so they claim. In al-Qaeda's view, dividing secular and religious authority as Kemal's government did in 1924 was an attack on God's divine plan, hence its goal of reestablishing a Muslim caliphate—this time on a global scale.

✦

Mustafa Kemal Ataturk died on November 10, 1938, at the age of 57. In 1934 surnames became compulsory in Turkey, which enabled Turks to produce a comprehensible phone book and simplify record-keeping. Kemal chose his last name: Ataturk, meaning Father of Turks. He had no natural children of his own though he adopted and supported several over the years. He adamantly rejected Ottoman imperialism and colonialism; as time passed the Republic of Turkey's Arab and European neighbors might see this break with the sultan's oppressive legacy as a sign that new relationships, based on common interests and respect, were possible. His real legacy was to leave behind him the structure of a democracy, not a dictatorship.[9]

In 1993 a woman and a trained economist, Tansu Ciller, became prime minister of Turkey. But in the twenty-first century the "war of the veil" continues, and not only in the Middle East. In July 2010 France's National Assembly, the inspiration for Turkey's parliament, banned the full-face Islamic veil.

In he treatise *On War*, Clausewitz wrote, "Even the ultimate outcome of a war is not always to be regarded as final. The defeated state often regards the outcome as a transitory evil."[10] Clausewitz was addressing nation-states; yet the insight describes any people inspired by ideals for which they are willing to fight.

The struggle for Turkey's soul continues. Typically, commentators identify two sides in this struggle. There are the Kemalists whose supporters believe they continue Ataturk's reforms. Their political party is the Republican Peoples Party (CHP), which was founded by Ataturk. Their critics, however, damn these Kemalists as antidemocratic, and see them as the "old guard" hardline secularists who run Turkey's "Deep State," a nefarious world of corruption and manipulation tied to the Turkish military. As Turkish area specialist Gerald Robbins points out, the democratic structure Ataturk created and modernization process he began used the military as its "necessary instrument." The military often forwarded modernization by "diktat instead of discourse."[11]

The Justice and Development Party (AKP) established in the first decade in the twenty-first century exemplifies the second side. AKP leaders describe themselves as Muslim moderates who believe religious values will halt Turkey's slide into corruption. Their critics claim the AKP is a stealth militant Islamist organization whose real goal is a state run by religious cultists.

A third side exists, one which harries all nations but particularly those vexed by deep internal divisions: the destructive energy of anarchy. In the first decades of this century, a range of violent ethnonationalist organizations, nonstealthy religious extremists, and radical leftist political splinter groups express this dark force within Turkey.

Ali Aslan, Washington correspondent for Turkey's *Zaman* newspaper, argues the AKP is led by Muslims who wish to engage the modern world:

> The primary struggle within Turkey is not between Islam and secularism, but rather between a militaristic pseudo-autocracy and liberal democracy.... The principles of Mustafa Kemal Ataturk loomed large in the minds of the young officers who spearheaded the 1960 coup, and Turkey's military class continues to justify its stance in the name of Turkey's founding father. But Ataturk was essentially a pragmatic reformer whose main goals were modernization

and integration with the West. The static, statist, and militarist instincts of Turkey's old guard have only slowed progress toward these objectives. The notion of the "untouchable state" preserved by the military and their comrades has changed...but much work still remains to be done. Despite the objections of his self-declared defenders, Ataturk would be proud.[12]

At the end of the twentieth century, corrupt practices in Turkey's government, financial, business sectors stunted economic progress. Bribes bought favored treatment. The politically connected received preferential contracts and loans. The AKP claimed religious values would help cure the moral laxity that seeded these practices.

Walter Russell Mead has argued that "eight years after winning its first election [in 2002], the AKP has started to resemble its political opponents." Turkey's prime minister Ragip Tayyip Erdogan, who also leads the AKP,

> it is said, makes all important decisions. Corruption allegations have become more frequent—as have the party leadership's attempts to use state power to deflect them.
>
> Many Turkish [military] officers see the current government trying to undo what Ataturk started, and they are not happy about it. Ataturk's western orientation was partly about cementing Turkey's place in the richer and more technologically advanced west; it was also about sealing Turkey off from the divisive conflicts in the east. Frustration with the west is understandably leading some Turks to look east; the results are more likely to vindicate Ataturk's view of Turkish national strategy than to refute it.[13]

In *The Kemalists,* published in 2005, Turkish journalist Muammer Kaylan examined the corruption and its consequences. Kaylan wrote that "political irresponsibility and greed,"and the "game of darkness and ignorance" persisted among Turkish elites despite "a multitude of potential danger signs caused by a militant Islamic reactionary movement."[14] By fall of 2002 Turkey "was a country with over sixty political parties and a dysfunctional government of loot-ers...a great number of have-nots were being alienated from the sec-ular reforms...The merchants of Islam, those exploiters of religion, the Communists, the Fascists, the thieves and looters embedded in the state and media used every means to manipulate the country's future....The nation was led away from its foundation in secular reform and ended up in total confusion about its destiny."[15]

Kaylan calls the AKP's 2002 electoral victory a disaster, but in truth, over six decades Ataturk's secular legacy had been betrayed. "Kemalism's most remarkable objective, its spirit of Western reforms, was neglected....That betrayal took the Turkish clock back to the days of the Ottoman Empire."[16]

Gerald Robbins argues that the Kemalist-Islamist divide has a demographic dimension with geographic roots. "Coastal Turkey" (particularly the Aegean coast) is a CHP stronghold: AKP strength lies in the "Anatolian Hinterland." Coastal Turkey is compara-tively wealthy and is culturally sophisticated. Robbins contends, "Coastal Turkey's proximity to Europe enables a close rapport with Mediterranean culture in thoughts and attitude." European proximity and cultural ties have influenced the CHP, which is one reason it philosophically resembles a European social demo-cratic party. "Conversely, the Anatolian hinterland maintains a poorer, more traditional setting," Robbins observes. "Islam resonates throughout this area, as do adjacent Persian and Arab influences, and it is here the AKP's Islamic concepts garner pas-sionate support." However, four decades of "rural to urban migra-tion" have politically "Anatolized" coastal Turkey's largest cities, Istanbul and Izmir, and the capital, Ankara, as well. These cities and their suburbs are now the scenes of intense secularist-Islamist political competition. Immigration shifted the political landscape; however, Istanbul remains in Europe and Izmir in its immedi-ate orbit. The next two decades may witness a "Europeanization" (i.e., a reculturization, to paraphrase Robbins) of the eastern

Anatolian immigrants living in coastal Turkey's cosmopolitan environment.[17]

✠

Ataturk believed that reason and logic provide the foundation for common values that all nations and cultures may share and respect. This is a grand and affirmative ideal, of course, and Ataturk, as an experienced combat soldier, was well aware that the world as it is and as it will be treats such ideals harshly. It is, however, as Andrew Mango notes, "an ideal that commands respect."[18]

But it does more than command respect, it empowers. The liberating appeal of what Ataturk regarded as common human values encourages Iraq's experiment in democracy. Those values energized the broad-based popular revolutions in Tunisia and Egypt in early 2011. These dramatic events suggest that pessimists underestimate the sustaining power of Ataturk's ideal.

Dr. Yuruk Iyriboz, who graciously translated several historical sources from Turkish into English as I researched this book, told me a personal story testifying to the power of Ataturk's ideal and his vision. In 1921, Dr. Iyriboz's father, Nihat Iyriboz, was the director of the School of Agriculture in Ankara. As the Greeks advanced through central Anatolia, Nihat went to Kemal and said that he and his students wanted to volunteer to fight. Nihat's family, like Kemal's, came from beautiful Salonika. Kemal also knew that Nihat was an educator and his students could read and write, unlike the vast majority of Turkish people in Anatolia. The pasha heard him out. Nihat told him, "We are going to join the forces fighting the Greeks." Kemal listened, and then replied, "No, we are going to beat them anyway. But we will need your students after our victory. I need you for what comes next."

What came next changed Turkey, for the better, and continues to inspire reformers and modernizers throughout the world.

Notes

Introduction: Winning Time

1. As World War I began, the Ottoman army lacked qualified officers to command divisions and corps. Staff College graduates, such as Kemal, often filled positions several grades above their rank. Erickson, *Defeat in Detail*, pp. 27–33. In chapter five of *A Military History of the Ottomans,* Uyar and Erickson note the shortage was rooted in two purges (1909 and 1913) conducted by Enver Pasha (Ismail Enver). Enver fired some 800 high-ranking officers because he believed they were too old to be effective.

2. Bean, p. 289.

3. Turks call the Dardanelles "Çanakkale Boğzi." Double names permeate histories of Gallipoli and Turkey's War of Independence. They present in sound bite form the question "Whose version of history?" The Turks called Hill 971 Koja Chemen Tepe; Chunuk Bair, Conk Bayiri; Battleship Hill, Düztepe (Flat Hill); and Baby 700, Kiliç Bayir (Sword Ridge). Ottomans entrenched on Battleship Hill and hid behind it, making it a target for Allied battleships.

4. Kemal did consult Colonel Halil Sami, Ninth Division commander, who suggested he take one battalion. Kemal took the regiment, leading two battalions. The regimental commander, Major Hussein Avni, followed with Third Battalion, Fifty-seventh Infantry. See Goncu and Aldogan, pp. 41–42.

5. Kemal, while critiquing Nuri Conker's assessment of Ottoman mistakes in the Balkan Wars, mentioned the failure of a regimental commander in the Battle of Boyalir (Bulair). Kemal said the officer led with his sword and should have led with his field glasses. Chapter 6 discusses the incident in more detail.

6. Drawn from Mango, p. 146. Mango quotes Kemal's 1917 report to the Turkish general staff. Unaydin's March 1918 interview with Kemal covers this incident.

7. Ibid. Following this order, the First Battalion of the Fifty-seventh Regiment commanded by Captain Zeki assaulted the Australians on Battleship Hill, followed by the Second Battalion, commanded by Captain Ata. See Goncu and Aldogan, pp. 41–42.

8. Clausewitz, p. 100.

9. Ibid., p. 101.

10. Ibid., p. 102.

11. Ibid.

12. Gawrych, "Kemal Ataturk's Politico-Military Strategy," p. 319.

13. Hallett, "A Landslide for Ataturk?"

14. McLaughlin, *The McLaughlin Group*. McLaughlin was responding to Lawrence O'Donnell's suggestion that Mahatma Gandhi was the "Person of the Full Millennium." Guests Michael Barone had suggested James Madison, Eleanor Clift suggested Charles Darwin, and Tony Blankley suggested Winston Churchill.

15. Clausewitz, p. 87.

16. "Nomination Database—Peace," Nobelprize.org.

17. Bay, "A Strategic Lunch."

18. Lerner and Robinson, p. 26.

Chapter 1: Rumelia

1. The source of this phrase is disputed. In 1854 Czar Nicholas I purportedly said that when dealing with the Ottoman Empire, Europe had a "sick man on its hands." Temperley, p. 272.

2. Bernard Lewis's book *What Went Wrong?* published in 2001 after al-Qaeda's 9/11 attacks, addressed Islamic political decay. An essay drawn from the book appeared in the *Atlantic Monthly*'s January 2002 issue and provides essential background. In it Lewis writes, "In the course of the twentieth century it became abundantly clear that things had gone badly wrong in the Middle East—and, indeed, in all the lands of Islam. Compared with Christendom, its rival for more than a millennium, the world of Islam had become poor, weak, and ignorant. The primacy and therefore the dominance of the West was clear for all to see, invading every aspect of the Muslim's public and even—more painfully—his private life. Muslim modernizers—by reform or revolution—concentrated their efforts in three main areas: military, economic, and political. The results achieved were, to say the least, disappointing." Lewis notes, "Turks could lay the blame for the stagnation of their civilization on the dead weight of the Arab past, in which the creative energies of the Turkish people were caught and immobilized."

3. Ottomans called Russia a Western power. Sublime Porte refers to the main gate of Constantinople's Topkapi Palace and the grand vizier's offices; the term can refer to the foreign ministry or can serve as shorthand for the sultan's government. The grand vizier was the sultan's principal minister.

4. Sayyid Qutb, the Egyptian Muslim-Brotherhood intellectual whose philosophy guided al-Qaeda's Zyman al-Zawahiri and Osama bin Laden, recommended a harsher version of this remedy.

5. Mango, p. 32.

6. Kinross, p.14. The mother-son vignette seems too perfect, but Ataturk insisted he was quite young when he first told his mother he had military ambitions.

7. Ali Riza was a customs official at the Papaz Koprusu post along the Greece-Macedonia border. His first two sons may have died there. The area produced timber, and Ali entered the lumber business, possibly while still working as a customs officer returned to Salonika. See Mango, pp. 28–30.

8. A sixth child, another daughter, was born shortly after Ali Riza's death. She also died in childhood. Of Ali and Zubeyde's six children, two reached adulthood. Mango, pp. 28–30.

9. Interview with Ahmed Emin in the newspaper *Vakit,* January 10, 1922. Quoted in Volkan and Itzkowitz, p. 29.

10. Mango, p. 30.

11. Several sources indicate Greek bandits stole Ali Riza's timber. Banditry may have led to his business failure.

12. Greece became autonomous in 1829, independent in 1832. Serbia obtained de facto autonomy in 1817, formal autonomy in 1830, and independence in 1878. Bulgaria was freed from Ottoman suzerainty in 1878.

13. Ottomans called the Byzantine Empire "Rum" (Rome). Rumelia meant "land of the Romans" (Byzantines). Until the Turks conquered the region, "Rum" included western Anatolia. By the end of the eighteenth century "Rumelia" referred to Thrace and Ottoman southeastern Europe.

14. The school was controversial. Muslim traditionalists repeatedly threatened the schoolmaster's life. Turkish general Galip Pansiler attended it in the 1870s and in 1938 recalled the school had to be put under government protection. Volkan and Itzkowitz, p. 32.

15. Mango, p. 33. Ataturk mentioned his youthful embarrassment at having to wear ill-fitting garb. Discussion of his schooling and disagreement with his teacher are also from Mango, p. 33.

16. Major Kadri's son, Ahmet, attended the military school. Ataturk later indicated Ahmet's uniform impressed him. See Gawrych, "Kemal Ataturk's Politico-Military Strategy," p. 322: "When I saw him [Ahmet], I decided also to wear such a uniform. Then I observed officers on the streets. I realized the road to reaching this rank required entering the military secondary school."

17. Kinross, p. 14.

18. Froembgen, p. 32. Froembgen says Ali Reza also preferred European style clothing: Ali wore "a well-pressed European suit of a quiet pattern. He was serious, dignified, and careful."

19. Kemal also means "maturity"—someone mature and capable (and thus perfected) beyond his years.

20. In Turkey, prior to Ataturk's reforms, family surnames as such were not used. People were known by occupations or family nickname or as "the son of" their father. The tradition works fine in a tribal or small feudal society (an early medieval English barrel maker might be known as John the Cooper); it creates problems for a larger polity and definitely for a modern bureaucratic state (John the Cooper thus becomes John Cooper and enters the tax rolls and phone directory with this name). In 1934, Ataturk, as president of the republic, would introduce "name reform" legislation (Law of Surnames) to regularize Turkish names as in the West.

21. Volkan and Itzkowitz, pp. 36–37, quotes Aydemir as saying the other Mustafa became "a prosperous shipowner" in Istanbul, which indicates Aydemir had a direct source.

22. Mango, p. 37. Namik (Nama) Kemal died in 1888. Though Muslim, he considered the Islamic world's treatment of women (which included the practices of polygamy and concubinage) as being a major contributor to its backwardness when compared to the West.

23. Now Bitola, Republic of Macedonia.

24. As a political term, *enossis* means "union with Greece." In 1974 the Greek colonels' regime attempted to unite Cyprus with Greece. Turks saw this as a repeat of 1897 and Crete. The Treaty of 1960 with Great Britain, Turkey, and Greece guaranteed Cypriot independence and gave the three nations the right to intervene to protect their communities.

25. Kinross, p. 16.

26. Ibid., p. 17.

Chapter 2: Young Turks

1. Beyoglu and Pera are used interchangeably and refer to the borough and its districts. The military schools were in the Harbiye district. The old academies are now a museum; the barracks and former hospital at Tash Kishla are a campus of Istanbul Technical University.

2. Jewish merchants and Arab craftsmen also lived in Pera. In the early sixteenth century Spanish Moors fleeing the Reconquista settled in the quarter.

3. Sebastian de Vauban's classic essay on manning forts illustrates the necessity of training people to use technology. Vauban focuses on assigning competent officers to command garrisons, but the broader lesson is that advanced

military technology (whatever the era) is useless if soldiers cannot use it skill-fully. See Vauban, "Treatise on the Attack and Defense of Fortresses."

4. Zurcher, "The Young Turks," p. 2.
5. Kieser, p. 3.
6. Volkan and Itzkowitz, p. 47, quoting from an interview conducted by A. E. Yalman in 1922.
7. Mango, pp. 44–46.
8. Volkan and Itzkowitz, p. 49.
9. Kinross, p. 21.
10. The family had fought for the empire. Ismail's father, Marshal Mehmet Ali, was killed in action leading an army during the Russo–Turk War of 1877–78.
11. Atay, p. 27.
12. Kinross, p. 25. Mango, p. 51, quotes Ali Fuad as saying the initial issues of the newspaper were written and published while he and Kemal were at the War College. Kemal was the group's leader.
13. Kinross, p. 24.
14. Turkish Ministry of Press Broadcasting and Tourism, pp. 15–16.
15. Mango, p. 50.
16. Kinross, p. 25; Mango, p. 50. Mango indicates Nuri may have posed the problem as an uprising in the capital's immediate hinterland.
17. Mango, p. 54. Kemal was promoted to captain on January 11, 1905, to staff captain on February 5, 1905.
18. Atay, p. 28.
19. Ibid.
20. See Zurcher, *The Unionist Factor,* p. 32.

Chapter 3: First Assignments, First Revolts

1. The Murzsteg program prefigured other international peacekeeping mis-sions, like Bosnia and Kosovo in the late twentieth century. Under Murzsteg, the European powers sent foreign officers to reorganize and direct Turkish police units in an effort to protect their own interests.
2. The Sixth Army (Army of Arabia) was based in Baghdad. It controlled units in modern central and southern Iraq, Kuwait, and eastern Saudi Arabia (Al Hasa).
3. From 1877 to 1908, Ottoman armies had one or two cavalry brigades, with two regiments per brigade. Regiments had six squadrons; squadrons had a captain in command, a subcaptain, three lieutenants, and 152 to 156 troop-ers who were usually armed with a saber, a revolver, and a Winchester lever-action repeating rifle. Reid, pp. 81–82.

4. Atay, p. 32; Mango, pp. 58–60.
5. Atay, pp. 33–34. The predatory expeditions evidently disgusted Colonel Lufti.
6. The Hauran operation occurred in March and April 1905. Zurcher, *The Unionist Factor,* p. 32.
7. Atay, pp. 33–34.
8. Mango, p. 58.
9. Clausewitz, p. 106.
10. Mango, p. 60.
11. Ibid., p. 76.
12. The date is uncertain. Kemal went to Salonika in February or March 1906 and was a member of Vatan at the time. Lufti was sympathetic to Kemal's reformist politics.
13. Zurcher, *The Unionist Factor,* pp. 32–33.
14. Also translated as "Motherland and Freedom."
15. Aksit, p. 20.
16. Operations included the Aqaba Incident or Crisis, a boundary dispute along the Ottoman–Egyptian Sinai Desert frontier, pitting the Ottomans against the British. Many Turks interpreted the confrontation as a sign of increasing British hostility. It darkened Ottoman views of British Balkan policy. See Heller, p. 3.
17. Aksit, p. 20.
18. Ibid., p. 23.
19. Tahir died in 1925. He compiled a history of Ottoman authors and *The Encyclopedia of Turkish Sciences and Learning.*
20. Kinross, p. 32.
21. Volkan and Itzkowitz, p. 55.
22. Mango, p. 65. The rank is between captain and major.
23. Ibid., p. 66.
24. Zurcher, *The Unionist Factor,* p. 43.
25. Armstrong, p. 2.
26. Ibid.
27. Most of the men were under age forty. Enver was a year older than Kemal; he began his military schooling early.
28. Mango, p. 74. Ali Fuad later asserted Kemal advocated creating a Turkish nation state, not just restoring the constitution.
29. *Encyclopedia Britannica Dictionary,* "Macedonia," p. 222; Heller, pp. 5–7.
30. Mango, p. 77.
31. Hale, p. 35. Hale says two hundred joined Niyazi, a native of Resne, in the hills. He began with one hundred soldiers and seventy-five Mauser rifles.

32. Zurcher, *The Unionist Factor*, p. 43. Enver hid after learning he was to be recalled to Constantinople. He claimed he ordered the assassination of Lieutenant Colonel Nazim, one of the sultan's intelligence officers in Salonika who was investigating the CUP. Nazim was wounded in the attempt on June 11. Nazim also happened to be married to Enver's sister.
33. Zurcher, *The Unionist Factor*, p. 35.
34. Ravindranathan, p. 78, for likely dates.
35. Ibid., p. 71. To glimpse the chaos, see "Turkish General Slain," *New York Times,* July 19, 1908. It erroneously states that Osman Hidayet "was assassinated in the barracks...by an officer connected with the 'Young Turkey' movement." The dateline is "Saloniki, European Turkey."
36. Adivar, p. 258.
37. Zurcher, *The Unionist Factor*, p. 44.
38. Volkan and Itzkowitz, p. 63.
39. Ibid., p. 64. They mention despondent letters Kemal wrote while on the ship to Tripoli.
40. Tripolitania had two administrative units: Tripoli and the district of Benghazi. See chapter 5, pp. 52–53.
41. Mango, p. 83. The gold was for bribes. Hamdi Ertuna quotes Kemal as saying he received two letters from the committee and Kemal requested funds. One letter to Kemal said, "There is a revolt [in Tripoli] against Liberty." Ertuna refers to a letter from Haci Adit that included this: "The money you wanted is ready. We can give you 1000 gold pieces." Ertuna, pp. 11–12.
42. Mango, p. 84.
43. Simon, p. 19.
44. Aksit, p. 26.
45. Mango, p. 84.
46. Kinross, p. 40.
47. Qiao and Wang, pp. 132–63. Kemal in Tripolitania (Libya) succeeds in "subduing the other army through clever operations"—which Qiao and Wang note are not necessarily military.

Chapter 4: Counterrevolution, Army of Action,
and Its Aftermath

1. The Muslim religious leaders were usually called either *muftis* or *hodjas*. A *mufti* is a Sunni religious scholar. *Hodja,* a term of respect, may refer to the leader of a mosque or community.
2. Ravindranathan, p. 81.
3. Also called the March 31 Incident, based on the old Turkish calendar date.
4. Ravindranathan, pp. 276–77.

5. Mango, p. 88.
6. Ibid., p. 89.
7. Ibid., p. 87.
8. Aksit, p. 28. Army of Action is a popular translation of Operations Army.
9. Dwight, p. 244.
10. Ibid., p. 239. Tashkishla is also called "The Stone Barracks."
11. Mango, p. 89.
12. In 1912 Kemal translated Litzmann's *Instructions for the Conduct of Company Combat*. With these two translations "Mustafa made his name as a brilliant theoretician." Mehlhorn, p. 10.
13. Proposed June 18, 1883; see Baycan.
14. Mango, pp. 90–91.
15. Kinross, p. 47. Officers in rebel battalions concentrated on CUP politics and neglected their units.
16. Ibid.
17. Gawrych, "Culture and Politics of Violence," p. 322.
18. Mango, p. 91.
19. Gawrych, "Culture and Politics of Violence," p. 322.
20. In the 1920s Kemal appointed Fethi ambassador to France.
21. In World War I, Hirschauer organized the American-manned Lafayette Escadrille squadron.

Chapter 5: The Turco-Italian War of 1911–1912

1. In 1911 an express train took approximately 24 hours to travel from Constantinople to Belgrade. In 1939 the Orient Express from Istanbul to Belgrade took 22½ hours.
2. Also called the Tripolitanian War and, in Italy, the Libyan War.
3. Similarly, al-Qaeda intends to reclaim lost Muslim lands, and Chinese nationalists claim China exerts a natural hegemony in Asia. In 1912, the Greeks wanted to revive the Byzantine Empire.
4. *Encyclopedia Americana,* p. 175. Staley, ch. 3, states, "Banco di Roma established un-economic 'economic interests' in Tripoli at the urging and under the subsidy of the Italian government" and further asserts that "long before the Banco di Roma went to Tripoli, Italian statesmen of nationalist inclinations were definitely planning to take the territory."
5. Zurcher, *Turkey,* p. 105.
6. Childs, p. 25. Grand Vizier Hakki told Sevket to use the Tripolitania garrison in Yemen. Sevket asked Hakki to guarantee Italy would not attack. Hakki, with many personal ties to Italy, made the guarantee. Bennett, p. 21.
7. The German cruiser anchored in the Moroccan seaport of Agadir.

8. The title of a popular pro-war song in Italy, recorded by tenor Gilberti Averando, is an example of cultural propaganda. Italian soldiers would soon learn that Libya was not beautiful. Bennett, p. 6.

9. Italy, as a member of the Triple Alliance with Germany and Austria-Hungary, was Germany's ally. Some Italians believed Germany sought a coaling station in North Africa. *Encyclopedia Americana* assessment, p. 175. In December 1911 the sultan permitted a shift west in the Anglo-Egypt border. French troops occupied the Djenat oasis in southwestern Libya.

10. Italy considered an attack on the Dardanelles in November 1911, but Russia objected.

11. Abbott, p. 112. Muslim religious ties, however, were important. Senussi were a Sufi Muslim religious movement or order founded in 1837. The Senussi "Bedouin of Cyrenaica" became a "politico-religious movement" that "had a tribal system which embraced common traditions and a strong feeling of community of blood" as its political foundation. See Evans-Pritchard, p. 10. Tribesmen belonging to the Senussi movement in North Africa began fighting the French in 1902.

12. The Italian naval attack sent a message about Balkan fragility that Austria-Hungary did not like; they warned Italy against further action in the Adriatic and Aegean.

13. This paragraph primarily relies on Beehler, pp. 16–20 (published in 1913), which draws on European sources. Beehler had served as the U.S. Navy attaché in Italy, Germany, and Austria-Hungary.

14. Ertuna, p. 29, has Italian and Turkish force estimates. Turkish artillerymen abandoned heavy field pieces but retreated with some mountain guns.

15. Mango, p. 101. Enver became a full major in 1907. He was the leading CUP officer in Tripolitania.

16. In Arabia and Palestine, T. E. Lawrence would use this stratagem against the Turks.

17. The Flying Tigers, the First American Volunteer Group in China, is analogous to this group. Although they were U.S. military pilots, the veneer of "volunteer" was necessary in summer 1941 when they deployed to Burma. In 1911 the Ottomans worried that Britain and France would object to their strategy of fomenting tribal rebellion, for the insurrection might spread to their North African colonies.

18. Mango, p. 103.

19. Hermann, p. 341.

20. Bennett, pp. 22–23.

21. Ertuna, p. 41.

22. Ibid.

23. Ibid., p. 134; dates the letter as May 9 on the old Ottoman calendar.

24. Kinross, p. 60.
25. Ibid., p. 34.
26. Abbott, p. 90.
27. Ertuna, p. 63.
28. Sun Tzu, p. 52.
29. U.S. Special Forces soldiers advising Northern Alliance insurgents fighting the Taliban in fall 2001 in Afghanistan would face a similar circumstance.
30. Ertuna, p. 63.
31. Ibid.
32. Beehler, p. 47.
33. This concern could also apply to field artillery support. In an Ottoman night attack at Derna in February 1912, Italian field artillerymen "did not fire their guns because they thought they might hit their own soldiers." Ertuna, p. 115.
34. Ibid., pp. 105–6.
35. Simon, p. 22.
36. Ertuna, p. 103. Sun Tzu, pp. 111–15, says intelligence gathering and assessment is how to "perceive" the enemy.
37. Ertuna, p. 139.
38. Ibid., p. 101.
39. Ibid., p. 95.
40. Ibid., p. 115.
41. Ibid., pp. 96, 117, 135.
42. Ibid., p. 105.
43. Kemal's letter says the date was January 4, likely on the Julian calendar. Kemal indicated the wound was bad enough to send him to the hospital facility in the desert. He told Kerim he became commander at Derna February 19; most sources say March 3 or 6.
44. Ertuna, pp. 118–19. The west wing was Nuri's command.
45. Ibid., p. 119.
46. Conker, pp. 103–4.
47. Ertuna, p. 120.
48. Ibid., p. 135.
49. Ibid., p. 105.
50. Beehler, p. 48.
51. Ibid., p. 106.

Chapter 6: The Balkan Wars

1. This summary draws on the entirety of Erickson's *Defeat in Detail*.
2. Kinross, p. 65.
3. Armstrong, p. 36.

4. Kinross, p. 66. Mango, p. 115, says Kemal met his friend Salih, who also came from Salonika, in a reading room, and provides a less poetic rendition of Kemal's outburst: "How could you leave Salonika, that beautiful home town of ours?" Turkish refugees suffered greatly in the flight from western Thrace as did Greek refugees fleeing eastern Thrace.

5. Ataturk, pp. vi–vii.

6. Erickson, *Defeat in Detail*, p. 63, and war plan 5, pp. 63–64. The Ottomans deployed 385 battalions in the east, 273 battalions in the west; the Balkan League fielded 556.

7. The CUP advocated Ottoman reinvigoration, not decline. In July 1912 the Liberal Union (also called the Freedom and Accord party) replaced the CUP government. The CUP's failure to win in Tripolitania cost it political support. By 1912 the CUP "seemed a spent force, relying on an increasingly authoritarian army and responsible for the alienation of Britain and France," Strachan, p. 656. The CUP had curbed parliamentary power in favor of centralizing power in the executive, which angered many CUP members who had fought for the opposite. In power, the Liberal Union government (and the sultan) repressed the CUP. The First Balkan War began, temporarily suspending the internecine struggle. These divisive events set the stage for the January 1913 assassination and coup.

8. Erickson claims that "the Ottoman Western Army's strategy for the defense of its operational area attempted to retain as much key terrain as possible for both political and emotional reasons." *Defeat in Detail*, pp. 201–2. Kosovo and the Sanjak of Novi Bazar (the Sanjak in modern Serbia and Montenegro) were "indefensible" and the Serbian Third Army took Novi Bazar October 23, 1912. The Kosovo force (the Pristina Detachment) consisted of two reserve infantry regiments—token resistance when three Serb divisions attacked, but still a waste of troops.

9. Erickson, *Defeat in Detail*, p. 65.

10. Atay, p. 54.

11. Ibid.

12. Erickson, *Gallipoli*, pp. 2–5.

13. Atay, p. 55.

14. Aksin, p. 77. Yakup Cemil was an army officer and ethnic Circassian who had served with Enver, most recently in Cyrenaica, and had traveled to Egypt on the same boat as Kemal. Cemil may have been one of Enver's bodyguards; by reputation he was a CUP "gangster." Enver had personal and political influence with the sultan and was engaged to an Ottoman princess, Naciye, whom he married in 1914.

15. Erickson, *Defeat in Detail*, pp. 251–59.

16. Armstrong, p. 39.

17. Erickson, *Defeat in Detail,* p. 255.
18. Ibid., pp. 252–59, summarizes planning, unit deployments, and movements.
19. Ibid., p. 258.
20. Erickson, *Gallipoli,* p. 6.
21. Erickson, *Defeat in Detail,* p. 259.
22. Ibid., p. 264.
23. Ibid., p. 267, and Battle of Sarkoy, pp. 259–72. Erickson praises Enver's handling of the evacuation.
24. Ibid., pp. 282–84.
25. Ibid., p. 284.
26. Ibid., pp. 317–28.
27. Atay, pp. 59–60.
28. Ataturk, pp. 7–9. The office Kemal reviewed in 1911 was that of Kara Tahsin Pasha and his staff.
29. Erickson, *Defeat in Detail,* p. 225, has the November 8, 1912, Salonika surrender protocol.
30. Ataturk, pp. 16–17. Doğan Arslan refers to Dohan Anslan Point with "yellow sloping cliffs," which lies on the eastern side of the coast at the neck of the Gallipoli Peninsula. About six kilometers east-southeast of Boyalir, the point is fifteen kilometers up the coast from the town of Gallipoli. Bulgarian lines were approximately two kilometers east-northeast of Boyalir and crossed the peninsula. This would make the Dohan Anslan cliffs a frontline position on February 8, 1913. The ridge behind the cliffs runs up to one of the two hills the Bulgarians used as defensive linchpins. See "The Black Sea Pilot," p. 55.
31. George Gawrych, in an unpublished paper delivered in Boston in 2010, argues, "Intellect helps direct an army in war and guides officers in taking initiative. Conscience calls forth the highest ideals of the profession, including patriotism and religious faith. A careful reading of the Ottoman original [of Nuri's lectures] published in 1918 shows the passion behind these two concepts in Mustafa Kemal's thought and character."

Chapter 7: The Great War Erupts

1. Kemal's "exile" was at the direction of Ismail Enver, who wielded tremendous power and became minister of war in January 1914, promoting himself to full colonel then general the same month. On March 1, 1914, Kemal was promoted to lieutenant colonel.
2. Kinross, pp. 71–72, 76.
3. Atay, p. 62.
4. Kinross, p. 69.

5. In 1914 Kemal told Nuri Conker the Bulgarians wanted Edirne. Still, the Bulgarian goal of an understanding with a former adversary, if not an alliance, was an objective the Ottomans shared. It played a role in Ali Fethi's assignment as ambassador. Fethi chose to resign his commission and take a political job. He became secretary general of the CUP and immediately confronted Enver, who had formed a guerrilla force in western Thrace. Fethi did not want to pay the force or any of Enver's private gangs. Mehmed Talat, serving as minster of the interior, suggested Fethi become ambassador to Bulgaria. Lieutenant Colonel Ahmet Cemal agreed and told Fehti the CUP government had "decided to court Bulgaria as a counterweight to Greece," Mango, p. 124. Enver's gangs eventually joined his Special Organization, a covert operations group loyal to him, whose goal was "to promote CUP objectives among Muslims outside the Ottoman state, and repress CUP enemies within it," Mango, p. 102.

6. Corinne, widow of Kemal's friend Omer Lutfu, who was killed during the Balkan War, held musical performances in her home in Pera, near the War College. She was an Istanbul sophisticate, avowed modernizer, and art lover. Kemal admired Corinne and her sister, Edith, and visited them both in 1913 prior to his assignment in Sofia. Their father was a doctor from a family of Italian origin. See Mango, pp. 122, 205.

7. Ibid., p. 129.

8. Atay, p. 63.

9. Mango, p. 129.

10. The violent sideshows indicated this war would be fought on a larger scale than any prior conflict.

11. German ambassador to the Sublime Porte, Hans von Wangenheim, wrote these words.

12. Strachan, p. 669.

13. Erickson, *Ordered to Die,* p. 19.

14. Strachan, p. 670.

15. Kinross, pp. 78–79. Turkey and Bulgaria negotiated a nonaggression treaty, signed August 6, 1914.

16. Strachan, p. 685.

17. Mango, p. 137.

18. Aksin, p. 96. Ahmet Cemal was naval minister and he claimed he was not consulted. Strachan suggests that Enver hid critical information from other members of the cabinet. See Strachan, p. 669.

19. The British-built *Resadiye* dreadnought had ten 13.5-inch guns. The *Sultan Osman* had fourteen 12-inch guns in seven turrets. Though Enver and Cemal used the seizure to inflame public sentiment, Churchill was either prescient or British intelligence well-informed regarding Enver's skullduggery. Churchill made the decision under pressure; a Turkish crew had arrived in Britain on July

27, 1914, to take control of the *Sultan Osman*. A contract clause did permit cancellation in the event of war, but facts rarely deterred Enver. Gray, p. 391.

20. Carlyon, p. 45. What a terrific pun—the German national anthem is "Deutschland Uber Alles" ("Germany above Everything").
21. Aksin, p. 96.
22. Carlyon, p. 47. The Ottomans had been defending the Straits for centuries. Seddulbahir (Sea Barrier) castle was built in 1659. It was not a complete relic; the position had been upgraded.
23. Strachan, p. 678.
24. Mango, p. 137.
25. Strachan, p. 685.
26. Mango, p. 139.
27. Atay, p. 69.
28. Ibid.
29. Ibid.
30. Ibid. Kinross differs, p. 84.

Chapter 8: Gallipoli

1. Erickson, *Gallipoli,* pp. 31–32. The Nieteenth would soon receive the Seventy-second and Seventy-seventh Regiments.
2. Mango, p. 143, who cites Izzettin Calislar's *Two Years with Ataturk.*
3. All data from Erickson, *Gallipoli,* p. 28.
4. Carlyon, p. 58.
5. That the Narrows' forts lie well within 15-inch gun range from an Aegean firing position off Gaba Tepe attests to the confined geography. Kilitbahir means "Lock of the Sea." Kilitbahir and the Çimenlik Castle across the Narrows at Çanakkale were built by Sultan Mehmet II in 1452.
6. Carlyon, p. 61.
7. Erickson, *Gallipoli,* pp. 16–29.
8. Brock, p. 91.
9. Fewster, Basarin, and Basarin, p. 56.
10. Quoted in Volkan and Itzkowitz, p. 86. Unaydin conducted the interviews in March 1918.
11. Fewster, Basarin, and Basarin, p. 58; the times are from Carlyon, p. 134.
12. Callwell, p. 43.
13. Liman von Sanders, pp. 64–66.
14. See chapter 1 for more details of the engagement.
15. Gawrych, "Rock of Gallipoli": "No Turkish regiment since has been allowed to wear its [the 57th's] number." Kemal's narrative is drawn from Unaydin.
16. Erickson, *Gallipoli,* p. 52.
17. See Introduction, note 3.

18. Callwell, p. 96.
19. Erickson, *Gallipoli,* p. 53.
20. Ibid., p. 55.
21. Bean, p. 289.
22. Ibid., p. 296.
23. Erickson, *Gallipoli,* p. 56, quoting Churchill's *World Crisis.*
24. The paragraph draws on Erickson, *Gallipoli,* pp. 57–65.
25. Erickson, *Gallipoli,* pp. 101–9.
26. Armstrong, p. 52.
27. Fewster, Basarin, and Basarin, p. 78.
28. Erickson, *Gallipoli,* p. 109.
29. Mango, pp. 149–50.
30. Kinross, p. 100.
31. Liman von Sanders, pp. 85–86. Erickson says Kemal had made this recommendation, *Gallipoli,* p. 156.
32. Liman von Sanders, p. 92.
33. Cameron, p. 19.
34. Ibid., pp. 20–21.
35. Ibid., p. 22.
36. Ibid., pp. 17–19, has the Commonwealth assessments.
37. A ravine entering a salt lake east of Suvla Bay; an ANZAC cemetery now lies near it.
38. Liman von Sanders, p. 86.
39. Mango, p. 151.
40. This description summarizes Erickson, *Gallipoli,* pp. 157–63.
41. Ibid., pp. 159–68.
42. Unaydin, third conversation.
43. Ibid. Some commentators call the watch story "popular tradition," but several witnesses attested to the incident.
44. Erickson, *Gallipoli,* p. 166.
45. Liman von Sanders, p. 90.
46. Fewster, Basarin, and Basarin, pp. 105–6.
47. Mango, p. 153.
48. Erickson, *Gallipoli,* pp. 182–83; see also pp. 228–29.
49. Mango, pp. 153–56.
50. Ibid., pp. 157–61.

Chapter 9: Eastern Front, 1916, to Palestine, 1918

1. Erickson, *Ordered to Die,* pp. 120–21.
2. Lengyel, p. 65.
3. Erickson, *Ordered to Die,* pp. 120–37.

4. Mango, p. 160.
5. Kinross, p. 116.
6. Lake Van was ancient Armenia's blue gem. Ethnic Armenians still lived in some of the region's towns after World War I, however, in 1915 many Armenians either fled to seek safety with the Russians or were driven out with fire, guns, and bayonets. Turkish nationalists fought Armenian forces in the area in 1920. In the twenty-first century this vicious historical debate continues unresolved: What happened? Did a genocidal massacre occur or a deportation of insurgents in the midst of war? Were the Christian Armenians waging an ethnic-based insurgency to aid the Russians, or were the Armenian citizens of the Ottoman Empire victims of ethnic cleansing (to use the 1990s Serbian term) at the hands of Muslim Kurds and Turks? The most accurate answer: all of the above. Mango notes there were "Armenian risings behind Ottoman lines" but deportations were a "brutal act of ethnic cleansing." This answer does not satisfy Armenians who demand reparations as well as apologies. It angers present-day Turks who accuse Armenians of recidivism and counter that during World War I Armenians and Russian massacred Turkish refugees. Hundreds of thousands of Armenians perished in cruel and tragic circumstances, and the deportations "deprived Anatolia of almost all its craftsmen." Mango, p. 161. Ataturk argued that there comes a time when demands for the return of ancestral territory must stop if a present peace and secure future are mutual goals.
7. "Atatürk'ün Diyarbakır'daki Kafkas Cephesi Komutanlığı, 1917" [Ataturk at Diyarbakir and the Caucasus front, 1917].
8. Erickson, *Ordered to Die,* pp. 131–37.
9. Ibid.
10. Mango, pp. 163–64. Mango quotes Ulig Igdemir's *Life of Ataturk,* vol. 1, 1988.
11. Erickson, *Ordered to Die,* p. 135.
12. In their controversial Ataturk biography *The Immortal Ataturk,* Volkan and Itzkowitz describe this period of Ataturk's life as "the peregrinations of a frustrated hero"; see pp. 95–105.
13. Ibid., p. 98.
14. Armstrong, p. 67.
15. Volkan and Itzkowitz, p. 99.
16. Ibid., p. 100.
17. Ibid., pp. 100–101.
18. "Palestine, Part II, Battles of Gaza and Yildirim Army Group."
19. Volkan and Itzkowitz, p. 102.
20. Ibid.
21. See "Mustafa Kemal Karlsbad'da." Carlsbad is now Karlovy-Vary in the Czech Republic. Its cold waters are said to have laxative properties, its warmer waters reduce bile and gastric secretions, hence the Viennese recommendation.

22. Volkan and Itzkowitz, pp. 103–6.
23. Or, Liman von Sanders believed that the information was up-to-date. Liman von Sanders, p. 264.
24. Cemal, p. 197.
25. See "The Arab Rebellion" in Cemal's postwar apologia, *Memoirs of a Turkish Statesman.*
26. Liman von Sanders, pp. 264–65. Kemal obviously told the German general that Enver lied to him.
27. Liman von Sanders, pp. 265–66, 273.
28. Ibid., p. 269.
29. Kinross, p. 138.
30. Erickson, *Ordered to Die,* p. 199.
31. Ibid., pp. 196–203.
32. Kinross, pp. 140, 142–43.
33. Mango, p. 181.
34. Kinross, p. 144.
35. Mango, p. 182.

Chapter 10: Anatolia Surrounded

1. Aksin, p. 119.
2. Ibid., p. 115.
3. Mango, p. 192.
4. Aksin, p. 119.
5. Mango, p. 207.
6. Ibid., pp. 200, 207, 208.
7. Zurcher, "The Young Turks," p. 564.
8. Ibid., pp. 565–68.
9. Mango, pp. 194, 209.
10. Ibid., p. 214.
11. Ibid., pp. 214, 215.
12. Ibid. p. 217.

Chapter 11: The War of Independence

1. Atay, p. 119.
2. Qiao and Wang, pp. 132–63.
3. Gawrych,"Kemal Ataturk's Politico-Military Strategy," p. 325.
4. Ibid., p. 326; Mango, p. 269. An American study commission concluded in October 1919 that Greek annexation of Izmir would be "contrary to the principle of respect for nationalities," Mango, p. 269. Woodrow Wilson had told the US Congress on February 11, 1918, that "all well-defined national

aspirations shall be accorded the utmost satisfaction that can be accorded them without introducing new or perpetuating old elements of discord and antagonism that would be likely in time to break the peace of Europe and consequently of the world," Wilson.

5. Mango, p. 225.
6. Ibid., pp. 225–26.
7. Ibid., p. 228.
8. Ibid., p. 230.
9. Gawrych, "Kemal Ataturk's Politico-Military Strategy," pp. 327–33.
10. Mango, p. 230.
11. Ibid., p. 234.
12. Ibid., pp. 234–37.
13. Ibid.
14. Ibid., p. 255.
15. Ibid., pp. 270–73.
16. Ibid., p. 295.
17. Ibid., pp. 288–95.
18. Smith, p. 129.
19. Kemal thought militia and partisan forces were unreliable. In December 1920 the Grand National Assembly ordered militias "to submit to the authority of the regular army." Gawrych, "Kemal Ataturk's Politico-Military Strategy," p. 331.
20. Smith, p. 117.
21. Greek domestic politics were in turmoil. Dimitrios Rallis formed the first post-Venizelos government and invited former King Constantine to return to the throne. In February 1921 Nikolaos Kalogeropoulos replaced Rallis. Dimitrios Gounaris became prime minister in April 1921.
22. Mango, p. 307.
23. Smith, p. 130.
24. Ibid., pp. 132, 190 (conference proceedings, Feb. 21, 1921), 192.
25. Ibid., pp. 198–99.
26. Mango, p. 311.
27. Ibid., p. 309.
28. Smith, pp. 225–27.
29. Kinross, pp. 308–10.
30. Smith, p. 227.
31. Orbay.
32. Gawrych, "Kemal Ataturk's Politico-Military Strategy," p. 332.
33. Ibid., p. 334.
34. Ibid., pp. 333–34.
35. Smith, p. 233.

36. Orbay.
37. Smith, p. 240.
38. Ibid., pp. 241, 252, 255.
39. Ibid., pp. 275–77, quoting E. A. Stravidis, "Behind the Scenes with the KKE."
40. Smith, pp. 284, 286.
41. Ibid., p. 287.
42. Gawrych, "Kemal Ataturk's Politico-Military Strategy," p. 337.
43. Kinross, pp. 354–55.
44. Gawrych, "Kemal Ataturk's Politico-Military Strategy," p. 337.
45. Smith, pp. 297–300. The initial attack (August 26 to 30, 1922) is called the Battle of Dumlupinar.
46. Ibid., pp. 303, 305, 306, 308, 310.
47. Gawrych, "Kemal Ataturk's Politico-Military Strategy," p. 325.
48. Clausewitz, p. 89, writes, "primordial violence, hatred, and enmity"; "the play of chance and probability"; and the "element of subordination, as an instrument of policy, which makes it subject to reason": these are a "paradoxical trinity" or "dominant tendencies." The people-government-army trinity is analogous.
49. Gawrych, "Kemal Ataturk's Politico-Military Strategy," pp. 325–26.
50. Toynbee and Kirkwood, p. 115.
51. Gawrych, "Kemal Ataturk's Politico-Military Strategy," p. 339.

Chapter 12: Ataturk at War in the Twenty-First Century

1. Aksin, pp. 111–12.
2. Kinross, p. 390.
3. TMPBT, pp. 215–17.
4. Ibid., p. 182.
5. Mango, p. 403.
6. Strachan, p. 682.
7. TMPBT, pp. 117–25.
8. Mango, p. 404.
9. Ibid., pp. 498, 534. In January 1923 Kemal married Latife Hanim (neé Usakligil). Latife was a well-educated, cosmopolitan woman from a wealthy Izmir family. The marriage did not last. They were divorced in August 1925. See Aksit, p. 262.
10. Clausewitz, p. 80.
11. Robbins, interview with author. Some material is taken from Robbins's unpublished lecture, "The U.S. and Turkey."
12. Aslan, "How Turkey Tamed Its Army." The 1960 military coup d'etat toppled a democratically elected government. The military regime tried and executed

former prime minister Adnan Menderes on what many believe were false charges (treason and abrogation of the constitution). It was the first of several military coups.

13. Mead, "Turkey Still Needs the West."
14. Kaylan, pp. 20–21.
15. Ibid., pp. 22–23.
16. Ibid., pp. 24–25.
17. Robbins, interview with author.
18. Mango, p. 539.

Bibliography

Abbott, George Frederick. *Holy War in Tripoli*. New York: Longmans, 1912.

Adivar, Halidé Edib. "Memoirs of Halidé Edib." In *Cultures in Dialog,* Series 4. Edited by T. Hefferman and R. Lewis. Piscatawy, NJ: Gorgias Press, 2004. Original edition published in 1926.

Aksin, Sina. *Turkey: From Empire to Revolutionary Republic.* Translated by Dexter Mersaloglu. New York: NYU Press, 2007.

Aksit, Ilhan. *Ataturk.* Istanbul: Aksit Kultur Turizm, 1998.

Armstrong, H. C. *Gray Wolf: Mustafa Kemal, An Intimate Study of a Dictator.* New York: Minton Balch, 1933.

Aslan, Ali. "How Turkey Tamed Its Army." *Foreign Policy Magazine,* May 28, 2010. http://www.foreignpolicy.com/articles/2010/05/28/how_Turkey_tamed_its _army?page=full.

"Atatürk'ün Diyarbakır'daki Kafkas Cephesi Komutanlığı, 1917" [Ataturk at Diyarbakir and the Caucasus front, 1917]. Isteataturk.com, April 5, 2010. http: //www.isteataturk.com/haber/4040/mustafa-kemal-8217in-ilk-savasi-trablusgar. Translation by Dr. Yuruk Iyriboz.

Ataturk, Mustafa Kemal. *Zabit ve Kumandan ile Hasb-ı Hal* [Interviews with officer and commander]. (Genelkurmay Askeri Tarih ve Stratejik Etut Başkanlığı Yayınları) [Turkish General Staff pdf of Minber Matbaası edition]. Ankara: Genelkurmay Basimevi, 1918. Pdf and translation courtesy Lieutenant Colonel Mesut Uyar, with translation and summaries by Dr. Yuruk Iyriboz, 2010.

Atay, Falih Rifki. *The Ataturk I Knew.* Translated by Geoffrey Lewis. Istanbul: Yapi ve Kredi, 1982. (Abridged version of Atay's *Cankaya.*)

Bay, Austin. "A Strategic Lunch with Mr. Rumsfeld." StrategyPage.com/Creators Syndicate, October 25, 2006. http://www.strategypage.com/on_point/20061025 22341.aspx.

Baycan, Nusret. *Ataturk Arastirma Merkezi Dergisi* [Ataturk Research Center Magazine 7, no. 19]. (November 1990).

Bean, C. E. W. *Official History of Australia in the War of 1914–1918.* Vol. 1, 11th ed. Sydney: Angus and Robertson, 1941.

Beehler, W. H. *The History of the Italian-Turkish War.* Annapolis: Proceedings of the United States Naval Institute, 1913.

Bennett, Ernest N. *With the Turks in Tripoli.* London: Methuen, 1912.

"The Black Sea Pilot: The Dardanelles, Sea of Marmara Bosporos, and Sea of Azov." H. O. Number 155, Hydrographic Office. Secretary of the Navy, U.S. Government. Washington, DC, 1920.

Brock, Ray. *Ghost on Horseback.* New York: Duell Sloan and Pearce, 1954.

Brosnahan, Tom. *Turkey.* 3rd ed. Hawthorn, Australia: Lonely Planet, 1985.

Callwell, C. E. *The Dardanelles.* London: Constable,1919.

Cameron, David W. *Sorry Lads, But the Order Is to Go: The August Offensive, Gallipoli, 1915.* Sydney: University of New South Wales, 2009.

Carlyon, Les. *Gallipoli.* Sydney: Pan Macmillan, 2002.

Cemal, Ahmet. *Memories of a Turkish Statesman, 1913–1919.* New York: George Doran, 1922.

Childs, Timothy W. *Italo-Turkish Diplomacy and the War over Libya, 1911–1912.* Leiden: Brill, 1990.

Clausewitz, Carl von. *On War.* Edited by M. Howard and P. Paret. Princeton. NJ: Princeton University Press, 1989.

Conker, Nuri. *Zabit ve Kumandan* [Officer and commander]. Istanbul: Tanin Matbaası, 1914. Turkish Military Academy pdf. Translations and pdf courtesy of Lieutenant Colonel Mesut Uyar, Turkish Army.

Dwight, H. G. "The Recent Capture of Constantinople." *Scribner's Magazine* (London) 46 (July–December 1909): 230–45.

El-Cheikh, Nadia Maria. *Byzantium Viewed by the Arabs.* Cambridge, MA: Harvard University Press, Harvard Center for Middle Eastern Studies, 2004.

Encyclopedia Americana. Vol. 27. New York-Chicago: 1920.

Encyclopedia Britannica Dictionary. 11th ed. Vol. 17. Cambridge, MA: Encyclopedia Americana Corp., 1911.

Erickson, Edward J. *Defeat in Detail: The Ottoman Army in the Balkans, 1912–1913.* Westport, CT: Praeger, 2003.

———. *Gallipoli: The Ottoman Campaign.* Barnsley, South Yorkshire, Eng.: Pen and Sword Books, 2010.

———. *Ordered to Die: A History of the Ottoman Army in the First World War.* Westport, CT: Greenwood Press, 2001.

Ertuna, Hamdi. *1911–1912 Osmanli-Italyan Harbi ve Kolgasi Mustafa Kemal* [The Turco-Italian War of 1911–1912 and Major Mustafa Kemal]. Ankara: Kultur ve Turzim Bakanligi Yayinlari (A.T.S.E.), 1985.

Evans-Pritchard, E. E. *The Sanusi of Cyrenaica.* London: Oxford University Press, 1973.

Fewster, Kevin, Vecihi Basarin, and Hatice Hurmuz Basarin. *A Turkish View of Gallipoli: Canakkale.* Richmond, Australia: Hodja, 1985.

Froembgen, Hanns. *Kemal Ataturk: A Biography.* Translated by Kenneth Kirdness. London: Jarrolds, 1936.

Gawrych, George W. "The Culture and Politics of Violence in Turkish Society, 1903–14." *Middle Eastern Studies* 22, no. 3 (July 1986): 307–30.

———. "Kemal Ataturk's Politico-Military Strategy in the Turkish War of Independence, 1919–1923: From Guerrilla Warfare to Decisive Battle." *Journal of Strategic Studies* (September 1988): 318–41.

———. "Rock of Gallipoli," (article) US Army Command and General Staff College Battle Command Studies, Combat Studies Institute, CGSC Faculty, http://www.cgsc.edu/carl/resources/csi/battles/battles.asp.

Goncu, Gursel, and Sahin Aldogan. *The Çanakkale War: The Homeland Is beyond the Trenches.* Istanbul: MB Publishing, 2006.

Gray, Randal, ed. *Conway's All the World's Fighting Ships, 1906–1921.* London and Annapolis: Conway Maritime Press, U.S. Naval Institute Press, 1985.

Hale, William M. *Turkish Politics and the Military.* London: Routledge, 1994.

Hall, Richard C. *The Balkan Wars: Prelude to the First World War.* London: Routledge, 2000.

Hallett, Bruce. "A Landslide for Ataturk?" *Time,* November 24, 1997. http://www.time.com/time/magazine/article/0,9171,987431,00.html.

Heller, Joseph. *British Policy towards the Ottoman Empire, 1908–1914.* London: Cass, 1983.

Hermann, David G. "The Paralysis of Italian Strategy in the Italian-Turkish War, 1911-1912." *English Historical Review* (Oxford University Press) 104, no. 411 (April 1989): 332–56.

Kaylan, Muammer. *The Kemalists.* Amherst, NY: Prometheus, 2005.

Kieser, Hans-Lukas. "Thinking 'New Turkey': Revolutionary Ottoman Groups in Geneva before 1914." Stiftung Forschungsstelle Schweiz-Türkei [Research Foundation Switzerland-Turkey], occasional paper. March 2008. www.sfst.ch/typo3/fileadmin/user_upload/dateien/OP_Kieser_08-03.pdf.

Kinross, Patrick. *Ataturk: A Biography of Mustafa Kemal, Father of Modern Turkey.* New York: William Morrow/Quill, 1992.

Lengyel, Emil. *They Called Him Ataturk.* New York: John Day, 1962.

Lerner, Daniel, and Richard D. Robinson. "Swords and Ploughshares: The Turkish Army as a Modernizing Force." *World Politics* 13, no. 1 (October 1960): 19–44.

Lewis, Bernard. "What Went Wrong?" *Atlantic Monthly* 289, no. 1 (January 2002): 43–45.

Liman von Sanders, Otto Viktor Karl. *Five Years in Turkey.* Translated by Colonel Carl Reichmann. Baltimore: Williams & Wilkins Co. for the United States Naval Institute, 1928.

Mango, Andrew. *Ataturk: The Biography of the Founder of Modern Turkey.* New York: Overlook, 2002.

McCullagh, Francis. *Italy's War for a Desert.* Chicago: F. G. Browne, 1913.

McLaughlin, John. *The McLaughlin Group.* PBS, aired January 1, 2000. http://www .ahmp.org/McLaugh1.html (excerpt of transcript with John McLaughlin's quotation), http://www.mclaughlin.com/transcript.htm?id=122 (entire transcript).

Mead, Walter Russell. "Turkey Still Needs the West." *American Interest* (blog), June 15, 2010. http://blogs.the-american-interest.com/wrm/2010/06/15/turkey-still -needs-the-west.

Mehlhorn, B. A. "Die Grundung der Turkei un die Rolle Mustafa Kemal Ataturks" [The founding of Turkey and the role of Mustafa Kemal Ataturk]. Hauptseminararbeit (paper). Norderstedt: GRIN Verlag, 2005.

"Mustafa Kemal Karlsbad'da" [Mustafa Kemal in Karlsbad]. Isteataturk.com. July 17, 2010. http://www.isteataturk.com/haber/5379/mustafa-kemal-karlsbad-8217da.

"The Nomination Database for the Nobel Prize in Peace, 1901–1956." Nobelprize .org. http://nobelprize.org/nobel_prizes/peace/nomination/nomination.php?action =show&showid=2046.

Orbay, Rauf. Quoted in "Quotations about Atatürk—Turkey." Republic of Turkey Ministry of Culture and Tourism. http://www.kulturturizm.gov.tr/EN/Genel /BelgeGoster.aspx?17A16AE30572D313AC8287D72AD903BEE15F7E276B12E FF0.

"Palestine. Part II, Battles of Gaza and Yildirim Army Group." The Yildirim Army Group. http://www.turkeyswar.com/campaigns/palestine2.htm.

Qiao Liang and Wang Xiangsui. *Unrestricted Warfare.* Beijing: PLA Literature and Arts Publishing House, 1999.

Ravindranathan, Tachat Ramavarma. "The Young Turk Revolution—July 1908 to April 1909: Its Immediate Effects." Master's thesis. Burnaby, BC: Simon Fraser University, 1970.

Reid, James J. *Crisis of the Ottoman Empire: Prelude to Collapse, 1839–1878.* Stuttgart: Franz Steiner, 2000.

Robbins, Gerald. Personal interview with the author. February 15, 2011.

———. "The US and Turkey." Unpublished lecture. "US Foreign Policy and the Modern Middle East" seminar cosponsored by the Foreign Policy Research Institute's Wachman Center for International Education and the American Institute for History Education. New Brunswick, NJ, Rutgers University, September 16, 2010.

Simon, Rachel. "Prelude to Reforms: Mustafa Kemal in Libya." In *Ataturk and the Modernization of Turkey,* edited by Jacob M. Landau, 17–24. Boulder, CO: Westview Press, 1984.

Smith, Michael Llewellyn. *Ionian Vision: Greece in Asia Minor, 1919–1922.* New York: St. Martin's, 1973.

Staley, Eugene. *War and the Private Investor.* Garden City, NY: Doubleday, Doran, 1935. http://www.gwpda.org/wwi-www/investor/StaleyTC.html#TC.

Strachan, Hew. *The First World War: To Arms.* Vol. 1. London: Oxford University Press, 2003.

Sun Tzu. *The Art of War.* Translated by J. H. Huang. New York: William Morrow, 1993.

Temperley, Harold. *England and the Near East.* London: Longmans, Green, 1936.

Toynbee, Arnold J., and Kenneth P. Kirkwood. *Turkey.* New York: Scribner's, 1927.

"Turkish General Slain." *New York Times,* July 19, 1908.

Turkish Ministry of Press Broadcasting and Tourism (TMPBT). *The Life of Ataturk.* Ankara: 1961.

Unaydin, Rusen Esref. *Anafartalar kumandani Mustafa Kemal ie Mulekat* [Conversations with Anafartalar Commander Mustafa Kemal]. Hamit Matbaasi, 1930. Originally published in the magazine *Yeni Mecmua* [New review] in three issues in the spring of 1918. Conversations are in Turkish at the Turkish Culture and Tourism website, http://www.kultur.gov.tr/tr/genel/BelgeGoster.aspx?F6E10F8892433CFFAAF6A A849816B2EFE0F4A247532D93A2. An English translation of conversation three is at http://www.kultur.gov.tr/EN/Genel/BelgeGoster.aspx?17A16AE30572D313 AC8287D72AD903BE8020F3B0746F34B3.

Uyar, Mesut, and Edward J. Erickson. *A Military History of the Ottomans: From Osman to Ataturk.* Santa Barbara, CA: Greenwood Publishing Group, 2009.

Vauban, Sebastian. "Treatise on the Attack and Defense of Fortresses." In *The Art of War in World History,* edited by Gerard Chaliand, 563–65. Berkeley: University of California Press, 1994.

Volkan, Vamik D., and Norman Itzkowitz. *The Immortal Ataturk.* Chicago: University of Chicago Press, 1984.

Wilson, Thomas Woodrow. "President Wilson's Address to Congress Analyzing German and Austrian Peace Utterances." February 11, 1918. http://wwi.lib.byu .edu/index.php/President_Wilson%27s_Address_to_Congress,_Analyzing _German_and_Austrian_Peace_Utterances.

Zurcher, Erik J. *Turkey: A Modern History.* 3rd ed. New York: I. B. Tauris, 2004.

———. *The Unionist Factor: The Role of the Committee of Union and Progress in the Turkish National Movement, 1905–1926.* Leiden, Netherlands: Brill, 1984.

———. "The Young Turks—Children of the Borderlands?" Turkology Update, Leiden Project Working Papers Archive, Department of Turkish Studies, University of Leiden, October 2002.

Index

refugees, 71, 115–16, 147, 179n4, 184n6
Republican Peoples Party (CHP), 164, 166
Reval Programme, 39
Riza Pasha, Ali, 27, 29
Robbins, Gerald, 164, 166
Robinson, Richard, 10
Rumania, 80, 87–8
Rumelia, 13, 16, 20, 28, 33, 36, 50, 56, 67–8, 72–3, 143, 171n13
Russia, xiv–xv, 3, 39, 51, 53, 55, 57, 87–91, 95, 112–19, 121–3, 145, 153–4, 171n3, 177n10, 184n6

Sabri, Eyup, 40
Said, Mehmet, 80
Sakarya, battle of (1921), 151–4
Salonika (Greek Thessaloniki), xiv, 10, 13–17, 19, 36–41, 43–5, 48–51, 56, 68, 69–73, 80–2, 136, 160, 167, 171n7, 174n12, 175n32, 179n4, 180n29
  cosmopolitanism of, xiv, 13–16
  ownership of, 16–17
  surrender of (1912), 69, 71–2, 81–2
Sari Bair, battle of (1915), 106–10
Sarkoy operation (1913), 70–1, 76–80
Savoff, Sava, 86
Sazlidere discussion, 107–8
Schlieffen Plan, 87
Sea of Marmara, 3–4, 76, 90, 96–7, 134, 154, 156
Second Army, 36, 38, 40, 44, 114–16, 118–22
Second Balkan War (1913), 80–1
secret societies, 16, 24–7, 35–6, 49
Secret Treaty of Alliance, 88
secularism, 8, 10, 161–6
Seddulbahir disaster (1914), 96–8, 182n22
Selanik Askeri Rustiyesi, 17–19
Senussi fighters, 60–1
September 11, 2001, 8, 170n2
Serbia, 16, 19, 52, 56, 68, 70–1, 80, 86–8, 136, 171n12, 179n8, 184n6
Seventh Army (Ottoman), 121, 123–9

Sevket Pasha, Mahmud, 44, 46, 49–50, 57–8, 76, 78–80, 176n6
Sèvres, treaty of, 9, 135, 147–9
sharia law, 9, 44
Sixteenth Corps (Ottoman), 9, 112, 113–19
Sixty-fourth Regiment (Ottoman), 103
Smyrna, 134, 140, 142–4, 149, 155–6
  great fire of (1922), 156
  occupation of (1919), 140, 142–4
Slavic people, xiv, 16, 19, 28
Souchon, Wilhelm, 89
Sultanate (Ottoman), xvi, 8, 14, 16, 23–5, 27, 29, 31, 33, 35–6, 38–40, 43–5, 47–8, 55, 76, 90, 112, 123–5, 134–40, 142, 145–6, 148, 160, 162–3, 171n3, 175n32, 177n9, 179n7,14, 181n19, 182n5
Sun Tzu, 60
supply routes, 3, 54–5, 67, 88, 110
Sykes, Mark, 126
Sykes-Picot Agreement, 126, 147
Syria, xvi, 32–4, 36, 38, 40, 122–3, 125–9, 135, 147

Talat, Mehmed, 38–9, 45, 75–6, 90, 105, 123, 125, 181n5
technology, 24–5
telegraph, 40, 47, 64, 114, 118, 134, 142–6, 150, 160
terrorism, 157
Third Army (Macedonia), 28, 36, 38, 40, 43–4, 48–9, 91–2, 113–16
Third Corps (Ottoman), 92, 99, 116, 118
Thirtieth Cavalry Regiment (Ottoman), 32, 34
Thirty Years' War, 47
Thirty-eighth Brigade (British), 109
Thirty-eighth Infantry Regiment (Ottoman), 50
Thirty-ninth Brigade (British), 109
Thirty-second Brigade (British), 108–9
Thirty-third Regiments (Ottoman), 103
Thrace, 3–4, 10, 16, 28, 38, 69–71, 73, 80, 88, 110–11, 114, 134–6, 142, 144, 148–9, 171n13, 179n4, 181n5